READING
AUSCHWITZ

ETHNOGRAPHIC ALTERNATIVES BOOK SERIES

Series Editors
Carolyn Ellis
Arthur P. Bochner
(Both at the University of South Florida)

About the Series:
Ethnographic Alternatives will emphasize experimental forms of qualitative writing that blur the boundaries between social sciences and the humanities.

The editors encourage submissions that experiment with novel forms of expressing lived experience, including literary, poetic, autobiographical, multi-voiced, conversational, critical, visual, performative, and co-constructed representations. Emphasis should be on expressing concrete lived experience through narrative modes of writing.

We are interested in the ethnographic alternatives that promote narration of local stories; literary modes of descriptive scene setting, dialogue, and unfolding action; and inclusion of the author's subjective reactions, involvement in the research process, and strategies for practicing reflexive fieldwork.

Please send proposals to:
Carolyn Ellis and Arthur P. Bochner
College of Arts and Sciences
Department of Communication
University of South Florida
4202 East Fowler Avenue, CIS 1040
Tampa, FL 33620-7800

Books in the series:
Volume 1, *Composing Ethnography: Alternative Forms of Qualitative Writing,*
 Carolyn Ellis and Arthur P. Bochner, editors
Volume 2, *Opportunity House, Ethnographic Stories of Mental Retardation,*
 Michael V. Angrosino
Volume 3, *Kaleidoscope Notes: Writing Women's Music and Organizational Culture,*
 Stacy Holman Jones
Volume 4, *Fiction and Social Research: By Ice or Fire,*
 Anna Banks and Stephen P. Banks
Volume 5, *Reading Auschwitz,* Mary Lagerwey
Volume 6, *Life Online: Researching Real Experience in Virtual Space,*
 Annette Markham

READING
AUSCHWITZ

Mary D. Lagerwey

PRESS

A Division of Sage Publications, Inc.
Walnut Creek • London • New Delhi

For information address:

AltaMira Press
A Division of Sage Publications, Inc.
1630 North Main Street, Suite 367
Walnut Creek, CA 94596
explore@altamira.sagepub.com

SAGE Publications Ltd.
6 Bonhill Street
London EC2A 4PU
United Kingdom

SAGE Publications India Pvt. Ltd.
M-32 Market
Greater Kailash 1
New Delhi 110 048 India

PRINTED IN THE UNITED STATES OF AMERICA

Library of Congress Cataloging-in-Publication Data

Lagerwey, Mary D. (Mary Deane)
   Reading Auschwitz / Mary D. Lagerwey.
   p. cm. – (Ethnographic Alternatives ; vol. 5)
   Includes bibliographical references (p.) and index.
   ISBN 0-7619-9186-7   ISBN 0-7619-9187-5 (pbk.)
   I. Holocaust, Jewish (1939–1945)–personal narratives–history and criticism. 2). Lagerwey, Mary D. (Mary Deane)–Journeys–Poland–Oswiecim. 3. Auschwitz (Concentration Camp) 4. Auschwitz (Concentration Camp)–Bibliography. I. Title. II. Series.
   D804. 195 .L34 1998
   940.53' I 8–ddc2 I   98-19715
                                                                 CIP

Editorial management by: Virginia Alderson Hoffman

Cover/interior design and layout: Kim Ericsson/Shooting Star Graphics

98 99 00 01 02 03 04 05 06 07   8 7 6 5 4 3 2 1

Contents

95743

Acknowledgments

Excerpts from *At the Mind's Limits* by Jean Amery (translated by Sidney Rosenfeld and Stella P. Rosenfeld, 81990) are used with the permission of Indiana University Press.

Excerpts from *Auschwitz and After* by Charlotte Delbo (translated by Rosette Lamont, 81995) are reprinted with permission from Yale University Press.

Excerpts from *Auschwitz: True Tales from a Grotesque Land* by Sara Nomberg-Przytyk (edited by Eli Pfefferkorn and David H. Hirsch, translated by Roslyn Hirsch, 81985) are used by permission of the University of North Carolina Press.

Excerpts from *Music of Another World* by Szymon Laks (translated by Chester Kisiel, 81989) are reprinted with permission from Northwestern University Press.

Excerpts from *Playing for Time* by Fania Fenelon with Marcelle Routier (translated from the French by Judith Landry, English translation 81977 Michael Joseph Ltd. and AthenFum Publishers) are reprinted with the permission of Scribner, a Division of Simon & Schuster.

Excerpts from *If This is a Man (Survival in Auschwitz)* by Primo Levi (translated by Stuart Woolf, translation copyright (c) 1959 by Orion Press, Inc., (c) 1958 by Giulio Einaudi editore S.P.A.) are used with permission of Viking Penguin, a division of Penguin Putnam Inc.

Portions of chapter two have previously appeared in the journals *Phoebe: An Interdisciplinary Journal of Feminist Scholarship* and *Contemporary Jewry: Journal of the Association for the Social Scientific Study of Jewry* and are used with permission.

Series Editors' Introduction
BY CAROLYN ELLIS AND ARTHUR P. BOCHNER

Ethnographic Alternatives publishes experimental forms of qualitative writing that purposefully blur the boundaries between social sciences and the humanities. Books in this series feature concrete details of everyday life. People are presented in them as complicated and vulnerable human beings who act and feel in complex, often unpredictable ways. As social agents, constrained but not controlled by culture, the characters in these books tell stories that often show a dazzling human capacity to remake and reform cultural narratives.

We encourage authors in this series to write ethnography reflexively, weaving details about their *own* lives and relationships into the stories they tell about *others*. The series' authors seek to share interpretive authority by presenting layered accounts with multiple voices and by experimenting with nontraditional forms of representation, including the fictional and the poetic. They try to stay open to surprise and to encourage challenges and revisions to their own interpretations. In these books, interpretive authority ultimately lies with the community of readers who engage the text. When these texts succeed, they encourage readers to feel, think about, and compare their own worlds of experience with those of the people they meet on the pages of these stories. In addition to stimulating a dialogue among academics across disciplinary lines, the books in the *Ethnographic Alternatives* series are written in a fashion that makes them accessible to a wider public audience, including people who can influence policy and implement social change.

In *Reading Auschwitz*, Mary Lagerwey seeks to understand the narrative accounts of people who experienced the Holocaust directly. She provides sequential readings of stories written by Holocaust survivors (and one victim), using each reading to build on and deepen our understanding of the one that came before. Readers enter the experience of Anne Frank, a female victim, and Elie Wiesel, a male survivor, who have written the most well-known accounts of the Holocaust. Lagerwey shows that the stories told by these two writers represent particular as well as universal experiences of the Holocaust. Her quest becomes to understand some of the particularities of the experience. By comparing exemplars of other male and female narratives, she coaxes readers to view stories of the Holocaust through a gender lens. She then complexifies the gender boundaries she has erected by taking into account other considerations in peoples' experiences, such as nationality, ethnicity, ideology, social class, status, and the situated complexity of each narrative. Readers accompany Lagerwey on her journey through multiple layers of interpretation and understanding. Each layer becomes more emotionally intolerable, until we finally enter the chaotic abyss of loss and despair depicted by these personal and collective stories, a place where our familiar categories have no meaning.

As readers, we are willing to go this far because we trust Mary Lagerwey as our cognitive and emotional guide. She willingly risks revealing her own thoughts and feelings as she candidly expresses what she has failed to learn as well as what she understands. Holocaust stories represent human experiences that cannot be explained in tidy categories that summarize what they mean. There are no words that adequately describe, no finished story that resolves. At the end, we find little peace. Yet our understanding of the importance of telling, listening to, and remembering the stories of the Holocaust has been reconfirmed. By remembering these stories, we make them part of ours, keeping the stories and the experiences they represent alive and accessible so that others can bear witness to the horror of the Holocaust and continue the search for understanding what happened and how. These stories force us to confront peoples' inhumanity to others, to vow that this kind of tragedy will not be repeated, and to appreciate the survival of the human spirit. Those are goals and values we must never forsake. *Reading Auschwitz* reminds us that this is so.

Preface

"History is what hurts"
–Fredric Jameson, 1981

*"History is not 'what hurts' so much
as 'what we say once hurt'"*
–Linda Hutcheon, 1989

Journal Entry: November 16, 1993

I am a pilgrim at Auschwitz.[1] I have taken an early morning train from Krakow to Oswiecim, where I visited Auschwitz I—now officially a "State Museum." There one can buy film, postcards, books of photographs, and even a hot dog. This visit is part of my doctoral research into personal stories from Auschwitz, so I try to make mental notes suitable for reporting back to my doctoral committee, none of whom have been here. But my mind refuses to play its part in the scholarly exercise. I walk around in a daze, remembering occasionally to take a picture. I've heard that many people cry here, but I am too numb to feel. The wind whips through my wool coat. I am very cold, and I imagine what the wind would have felt like for someone here fifty years ago without coat, boots, or gloves.

Hours later, as I write, I tell myself a story about the day, hoping it is true, and hoping it will help me make sense of what I did and did not feel.

All day I have been very much alone, by choice and internal necessity. I did not follow the signs and the crowds. Overwhelmed by juxtaposed images of death and commercialization, I recoil from being processed through such a place. Instead, I began by visiting

11

the Dutch National Pavilion, hoping to find traces of how my grandparents' country tells its story of the Holocaust. The exhibit covers the second floor of one of the barracks. Pushing a button at the bottom of the stairs offers me half an hour of artificial light. There are portraits of prominent Dutch Jews. Against a backdrop of a painting resembling a train signal covering the far wall, there is a sign directing trains from Westerbork to Auschwitz. Near the exit there is an enormous photograph of a girl at play, and a poem in Dutch, Polish, and English. The poem ends with these words: "Even after those fearful years Jewish children still laugh and play." Except for the train sign, the exhibit makes little direct reference to Auschwitz.

I leave to walk the three kilometers to Auschwitz II. Birkenau, by contrast, is almost desolate. I see a few signs for a suggested "visitors' walk" to what my brochure calls the 1967 "Monument Commemorating the Victims of Fascism." Across the fields I see a solitary group of students and the ruins of earth, train tracks, and buildings. The land is flat, with an occasional tree. I am dimly aware of bits of mud—perhaps mingled with ashes—sticking to my boots. I am enclosed by barbed wire fences on all sides. I dare not touch the wires.

I know very little about the lost lives, stories, and silences beyond stories of those who have stood where I am standing now. All I have are a few stories from this inner circle of hell that now sucks at my boots. I recall Primo Levi's words, "Death begins with the shoes." (1961, p. 29)

More than half a century has passed since the end of the Holocaust. Over the past six years, I have become increasingly aware of the stories of Auschwitz and its survivors,[2] and their significance for people like me—removed by time, place, and ethnicity from these events. Stories from Auschwitz converge on my consciousness from several sides. While a doctoral student in sociology at Western Michigan University, I occasionally visited the undergraduate Holocaust course my advisor teaches. I began to read more about the Holocaust, and talk informally with friends, family, and colleagues about what I was reading, and felt that I was simultaneously discovering new stories about the Holocaust and rediscovering some of my family's collective stories. I learned that other family members were also living more consciously within these stories. My mother, Marcia Lagerwey, was reading works by Dietrich Bonhoeffer, a German clergyman hung by the Nazis for his role in a plot to assassinate Hitler. For several years, my cousin Wallace Lagerwey has been arranging a Holocaust commemoration at Elmhurst College where he teaches German. When we learned of each other's interests, he invited me to attend. During a visit I made to my uncle's home, he showed me several books by Holocaust survivors he had recently read. I thought back to bits of family stories I'd heard about my paternal grandfather who, diagnosed with dementia, died in a Dutch psychiatric hospital sometime during Nazi occupation, and wondered about the details of his death. I had known historical facts about the Holocaust before, but not until I read many first-person accounts did I comprehend that people like me had lived and died at places like Auschwitz. These stories have brought me, as a reader, closer to encountering Auschwitz as those it was designed to destroy experienced and remember it.

Of course some of what I have seen, read, and thought has been in commemoration of the fiftieth anniversary of the Holocaust, but this does not fully explain the deeply personal connections I felt with some of the stories I encountered. These connections are rooted in my family's Dutch heritage, my own interests in women's stories, and questions I have about meaning in the face of suffering. My encounters with Holocaust stories have at times left me overwhelmed and numb, and at other times invaded my dreams. The atrocities of Auschwitz and the words of those who were there have become the raw materials of many of my own personal and intellectual stories.

When I listen to their voices and ask that others do the same, I feel that I honor the lives of Holocaust victims and work against the totalitarian subsumption of Auschwitz in which particularities of individual identity were all but obliterated. Survivor stories contain situational, contextual, and universal truths.[3] The victims of the Holocaust have a claim on my memories and language. They ask me to take my place in what Sara Horowitz, in *Voicing the Void: Muteness and Memory in Holocaust Fiction* calls the "chain of testimony" (1997, p. 224), to witness to individual stories of Holocaust victims, re-tell these stories, encourage others to read survivors' words, and situate myself in "anamnestic solidarity with the innocent victims of the past" (Siebert 1992, p. 29). They demand that I engage in individual and collective self-critical reflection on that which can never be made good again. I listen for words and silences from within the shadow of the tension between the unspeakable and the need to bear witness to that which no one was meant to survive.

I have frequently turned to other writers for words by which to approach the stories of Auschwitz. In reading Linda Hutcheon's work on language and representation (1988, 1989a, 1989b, 1993), and in conversation with her, I have come to better understand the juxtaposition of my own tears and suspension of feeling as I encounter these stories. Hutcheon's words also remind me that I am always at least one step removed from raw events and others' experiences. I can never wholly enter into the realities of these survivors' lives, for these tales come to me filtered through layers of time, distance, and story.

R. Ruth Linden's Holocaust writing, and her own reflections, have encouraged me to make transparent my struggles in reading these stories. In *Making Stories, Making Selves: Feminist Reflections on the Holocaust* (1993) she calls for a feminist ethic of honest reflexivity, a methodological map, in all social research. Her writings about lived experiences of Holocaust survivors and her own working through of the research process, guided me in using personal stories to better understand what the Holocaust has to say to me today. Linden tells of her earlier approach to Holocaust stories, in which she regarded them as unmediated historical documents. She then reflects upon her own story and intellectual history and re-reads the stories. Her inductive and reflexive methodology serves as a powerful model for reading personal Holocaust stories and encourages me to identify, examine, and critique my own readings.

It has been difficult and painful to grapple with these stories, and to disclose my emotions and numbness in interacting with them. It is easier for me to think and write abstractly about my encounters with the Holocaust, and harder to pierce my protective garb of academe and allow myself to feel the words of those of whom I write. It is infinitely more difficult to write of those feelings. I am by nature reticent to publicly discuss my feelings, and do not want to draw inappropriate attention away from the stories of the survivors to myself. I frequently ask myself, what right do I, a non-Jewish woman born eight years after liberation, have to merge these stories of the Holocaust into my own?

On the other hand, all attempts to write of how I've read these survivors' words in my usual analytic style—leaving myself out of the stories—failed to communicate my reading experiences. These earlier attempts were inconsistent with the demands with which these stories called to me to enter the lives of their authors. Perhaps my self-defined humility had merely protected me from touching the terrors of Auschwitz and letting them speak to me. But I also know that my own numbness faintly reflects the numbness of which survivors speak, and allows me to peer over their shoulders into the void of Auschwitz.

Without some distance and numbness, it would be impossible to write coherently of Auschwitz, but distance and numbness alone render survivors as impersonal beings, and ignore the relevance of the Holocaust for today. Sara Horowitz speaks to all forms of Holocaust literature. She challenges me to honestly confront my own "psychic numbness" (1997, p. 105) and recognize that honest Holocaust writing "enacts a kind of muteness in the very midst of an ongoing narrative" (p. 39).

In the pages that follow, my tale of reading survivor stories inevitably twists back and forth between intellectual analysis and reflection on how survivors' voices speak to me today. Stories of travel are woven into the larger story of reading. I have been reading countless books about Auschwitz, but they could not give me the embodied knowledge I needed to write about the experiences of its survivors. Each time I read their stories I glean new understandings of their lived experiences and my own reactions to their words, and each time changes the ways in which I live my own stories. To keep the readings from becoming too unwieldy, I have tethered them to three anchors, a somewhat artificial structure of three readings that I label gendered dichotomies, situated voices, and chaos.

OVERVIEW

Chapter One begins with several introductions. I introduce those survivors whose stories have most closely touched my own, and other writers whose thoughts form a framework for my readings. I also describe Auschwitz as the setting for these stories, and introduce themes of memory and story, silence and voice.

In Chapter Two I tell a tale of two stories, *Anne Frank: A Diary of a Young Girl* and Elie Wiesel's *Night*, that introduced me to the Holocaust. I reflect on these two life stories as the bases for much of public understanding, or collective memories, of Holocaust experiences. While Frank's and Wiesel's stories speak powerfully of the Holocaust and make its reality accessible, I also discuss my concerns that they obscure other stories. My doubts arise not over the legitimacy of Frank's and Wiesel's voices, but from the implicit—sometimes explicit—avowal that one male voice can represent survivors, and that a single female voice can represent young victims.

In Chapter Three I tell how I first read the stories of six Auschwitz survivors. I begin by exploring specific inadequacies of a single representative voice from Auschwitz. I organized this reading around familiar patterns of gender difference. A single story cannot speak for all survivors; the experiences of women and men at Auschwitz were not only separate, but qualitatively distinct. Women's stories tell of uniquely female experiences: pregnancy, childbirth, menstruation, amenorrhea. Moreover, women's stories speak more of emotional support, informal net-

works among prisoners, and close identification with their reproductive bodies. Men's stories more often emphasize isolation,
efficiency, official institutional structures, and tangible physical
assistance such as food.

In Chapter Four, I argue that the dichotomous gendered
reading presented in Chapter Three does not adequately cover
the complexity of survivor stories. It simultaneously grounds and
must be supplemented by a second reading. The first reading, in
fact, prompted me to listen for additional particularities–such as
social class and ethnicity–that complicate these writings. Survivors embed others' stories within their own stories, and tell of ways
in which they clung to or created new bits of identity by which
they could locate themselves. Chapter Four ends with a look at
ways in which Auschwitz frequently and systematically reversed,
twisted, and destroyed ways in which humans maintained their
identity and thus their dignity.

Chapter Five takes a closer look at the chaos of Auschwitz,
and the role of the grotesque in survivors' stories. Their voices do
not allow me to rest with thoughts of tidy conversational categories. The chaos of Auschwitz overwhelms and twists individual
existence into grotesque caricatures. In my third reading, stories
of Auschwitz tell of a world of totalitarian domination, where
"everything is possible." In the tumult of Auschwitz and in the
stories of its survivors, simple notions of multiple stories are
overwhelmed by a cacophony of voices resonating with the
bureaucratic violence that formed the essence of Auschwitz. Here
I find an inversion of hierarchies, loss of language and reason, and
hints of the subversive. The essence of the grotesque is degradation, contradiction, madness, and torture. It is a world of the bizarre,
the incongruous, and the irrational.

In the final chapter, "Reflections," I look back on reading
Auschwitz stories, and trace how each subsequent reading enriches,
complicates, and adds depth to my previous readings. I circle back
to my starting points: How do and should people today come to
know about the Holocaust? How has my life story become so
interwoven with these survivors' stories? How can we keep survivors' stories alive in our cultural memories?

Hannah Arendt has said that each of us is born into and lives within webs of stories and storytellers. This has become abundantly clear to me throughout the process of writing this book. I have a new appreciation for the countless stories that have been interwoven with mine. The webs of stories into which I was born emphasized the word, the life of the mind, and the worth of each individual story. My writing is born out of and sustained by this living heritage.

I especially thank those who have read drafts of this writing and given valuable suggestions. These include my sisters Renee Van Dyke and Karen Westra, my mother, Marcia Lagerwey, colleagues Douglas Davidson, Joanne Dogson, Martha Fakkety, Kathryn Kinnucan-Welsch, R. Ruth Linden, Gerald Markle, Maria Perez-Stable, Gwen Raaberg, Joan Ringelheim, Subhash Sonnad, and Joan Wendling; and Mitch Allen, Arthur Bochner, Carolyn Ellis, Erik Hanson, Virginia Hoffman, and Denise Santoro with AltaMira Press.

NOTES

1. I use the German names, Auschwitz and Birkenau (also called Auschwitz II) to refer to the death camps in the Polish towns of Oswiecim and Brezinka. The word "Auschwitz," once merely the generalized name of a town in Poland, is now equated with the concentration camp and customarily stands for the entire Holocaust. "Auschwitz" is often used in a metonymic sense, as a synecdoche, a part–particularly an important part–which signifies the whole. Theodor Adorno's dictum, that it is barbaric to write poetry after Auschwitz, is a widely quoted example of the same synecdoche.

2. The word "survivor" is problematic because, as some argue, no one really survived the Holocaust. I use the term "survivor" to indicate prisoners of Auschwitz who were physically alive after liberation, who in the words of Fania Fenelon, "came out with their lives" (p. 117), and I distinguish these individuals from those who died in the camps.

3. See Lyotard's *The Postmodern Condition: A Report on Knowledge* (1984) where he defines grand narratives as modernistic teleologic stories of universal truth, justice, and progress that claim descriptive and prescriptive legitimacy.

CHAPTER 1

Introductions

Journal Entry: July 10, 1996

I've returned to Poland to further explore the Netherlands National Exhibition at Auschwitz. I begin with a two hour individual tour of Auschwitz I. The guide tells me that during Nazi occupation, all Polish people within a 40 Km radius were expelled. I feel numb until I come to the displays of shoes, combs, and hair. My vision blurs, and I weep. I remember just two weeks ago carefully packing and re-packing for my trip, choosing just the right shoes and hair combs, practicing different ways to twist or braid my hair for the journey. The women who came to Auschwitz half a century ago must have done much the same as I had done only a few days ago. At this moment I know in my bones something of how the women who wore these shoes, combs, and hair lived, how they carefully packed the essentials they thought they and their families would need—plus a few aesthetic necessities.

Here in front of me now are practical shoes and favorites, sandals, and red pumps. Hair combs mix with other essentials for travel: brushes for teeth, hair, and shoes. Much of the hair is braided. I touch my own braided, tied back hair of which I am unreasonably proud, and feel panic at the thought of having it chopped off as

these women have—of having my head shaved. I have lost any
feelings of safety, any feelings of distance or basic difference
between these victims and myself. I feel extremely vulnerable.

AUSCHWITZ STORIES

Survivors tell us that their memories of Auschwitz are beyond telling. Yet the cumulative effects of their words point to the events themselves and give witness to their memories of that time and place. The stories of the few who survived come to us in many forms: visual arts, theater, music, oral histories (recorded and unrecorded), and the written word, and shape how I now think about Auschwitz. These artifacts of memories written by the women and men who were there have remained in my mind, seeping into my own memories, and into the stories I live, forming and re-forming my visions of the past and the future, and engulfed my being.

There are countless stories, told and untold, of Holocaust victims and survivors. Close to one and a half million Holocaust victims were children. The published material alone is overwhelming. The *World Catalogue*, for example, on March 7, 1998, had one hundred sixty entries for Holocaust diaries, one hundred thirty of which are in English. And there are numerous stories from Holocaust survivors, including hundreds from Auschwitz. As of 1990, the Archive of the Auschwitz Memorial had a collection of 2,744 accounts of survivors; 943 were memoirs, comprising more than 20,000 pages. Over one hundred individual memoirs have been published in English, and more are published each year.[1] Each story cradles within it the stories of others, particularly of the dead who cannot tell the stories of their last days. To whose stories do I choose to attend? To what form of story-telling will I listen most closely?[2]

I began reading personal Auschwitz stories for the ways they reflect and shape knowledge of the Holocaust in the United States today. I thus turned to those personal stories in the public domain of Holocaust literature in the United States. Although some of these survivors' stories are better known than others, the words of each have entered public stories about Auschwitz. Each is a cultural object and a collective representation (Griswold 1994; Durkheim 1915). I read first- person accounts that my doctoral advisor recommended. I searched my university and community libraries under categories of "Holocaust" or "Auschwitz" and "personal narrative." Thinking I had followed a clearly documented path of sociological sampling, I chose personal stories by six survivors: Jean Amery, Charlotte Delbo, Fania Fenelon, Szymon Laks, Primo Levi, and Sara Nomberg-Przytyk. I began with five tidy and interrelated criteria: (1) all have been translated into and published in English; (2) all were written after liberation by survivors of Auschwitz; (3) all have been included in Holocaust anthologies or course syllabi; (4) all–three by women and three by men–illustrate ways in which gender shapes stories; and (5) all are publicly available, either through bookstores or libraries. In keeping with these criteria I excluded transcribed interviews or taped testimony and works described by the Worldcat listing of published books as having fifty or fewer copies printed, and thus only limited accessibility. Through a sociological lens I thought of personal Auschwitz stories as texts of collective memory, texts that simultaneously embody gendered contrasts, multi-voiced complexities, and the chaos of Auschwitz.

These survivors are neither typical nor representative of Auschwitz prisoners. Less than one percent of all Auschwitz prisoners survived. Of these, far less than one percent have written and published memoirs available in English. The survivors through whose words I've learned about Auschwitz were intellectuals, skilled at meeting the world through their minds. Much as I am drawn to their articulate words, I know that their accounts cannot speak for the dead of Auschwitz. Doubtless the thousands of survivor interviews audio- and videotaped over the past decade by organizations such as Holocaust museums, the Yale University Fortunoff Archives, and the Spielberg Project represent a broader range of survivors.

The more I reflected on and tried to convey to others the formal reasons for my choices, the less adequate these criteria sounded. I realized that there were less formal, less tangible, and more authentic reasons why I'd chosen these works. The survivors whose stories I've included had come alive for me through their written words. I came to know them and to care deeply about them. As I stumbled through survivors' stories, I was especially drawn to voices that impressed me as particularly and courageously authentic. They refused to squeeze goodness out of evil, to valorize their lives, or to attribute their survival to superior coping skills. I identified with many in their reticence to put too many details of their lives into their writing.

I recognized that I had been attempting to learn more about the lives of Auschwitz survivors in a vain hope of resolving some of my own theological struggles with suffering and meaning. The more I read of survivors' lives, the more ashamed I felt for using their suffering in this way, and I recognized a respect for and an affinity with their refusal to resolve that which cannot be resolved. Their stories brought me back to memories of my own losses—obviously trivial in comparison, but resonating with the same truths. When my father died at age fifty-two—a painful death of cancer—some twenty years ago, I felt insulted by demands that I believe this was God's will, that good would come from his suffering and from my loss. The survivors who made me weep with them, and to whose stories I went again and again, echoed what I already knew: that any healing that follows horror can only be arrived at through painful honesty, and that some endings cannot be made right. What began as a sociological comparison of style and themes "within and between" stories by equal numbers of female and male survivors evolved into a personal story about the integrity of lives, deaths, and stories. One thing that has remained constant has been my choice of survivors. The following is a brief introduction to these six survivors and to their writings.

Jean Amery (1912–1978)

Jean Amery's work, *At the Mind's Limits* (1990)[3], is a collection of essays. While not filled with graphic depictions of Auschwitz, it disturbed me the most of any Holocaust writing I've encountered. It is eloquent, indisputably honest, and infused with existential despair for all of humanity. I could read no more than an

essay a week without feeling too overwhelmed to think of anything else, and I could not escape his world to offer an honest
rebuttal. My own joy in living felt like fleeting denial. Amery's
writing brought me to the uncomfortable acknowledgment that I
could not face the truths of Auschwitz for a sustained time without
surrendering to conclusions of hopelessness.

Jean Amery tells little of the details of his life in his collection
of essays. In the foreword, translator's note, and afterword, others
outline the facts that frame his life story. Amery was an Austrian
of Jewish descent. An only child, he was born in Vienna on October
31, 1912, as Hans Maier. His mother was Jewish and Roman
Catholic, but never identified herself as Jewish. His Jewish father,
whose family had lived in the Vorarlberg town of Hohenems since
the 17th century, was killed in World War I fighting for the Germans.
Amery grew up in the resort town of Bad Ischl in the
Salzkammergut, where his mother managed an inn. Upon com-
pleting his gymnasium education, Amery moved to Vienna, where
he studied philosophy and literature. In 1937, against his mother's
wishes, he married an Eastern European Jew from Graz. The two
fled the Nazis to Brussels in 1938. Amery's mother died in Vienna
in 1939 without ever experiencing Nazi persecution. Amery was
arrested by the Belgians in 1940 as a German alien and spent time
in several prisons, including Gurs from which he escaped in 1941.
He was arrested again in 1943 by the Gestapo for his work in the
Belgian resistance. When Gestapo officers at the Breendonk reception camp discovered that Amery was Jewish, and not a German
deserter, they sent him to Auschwitz, where he was imprisoned
for one year, then sent to Buchenwald, and finally Bergen-Belsen,
from which he was liberated in 1945. His wife had died of a heart
condition while he was in Auschwitz. Amery was never a practicing Jew. He thought of himself as "Christian" until the Nuremberg
Laws defined him as Jewish because his parents were of primarily
Jewish lineage. He thereafter defined himself as a "catastrophe"
or "Holocaust" Jew (Young 1988, pp. 109, 127).

After liberation, Amery was a cultural correspondent for several German radio stations and a political and literary writer for
Swiss publications. He remarried, this time to a Jewish woman

from Vienna who had been in the United States during the Holocaust. They lived in Brussels, Belgium, until his suicide in 1978.

Amery's publications available in English include *At the Mind's Limits* (1966, 1990, translated from the German *Beyond Guilt and Atonement*, 1964), *Preface to the Future: Culture in a Consumer Society* (1964), *On Aging* (1969), and *Radical Humanism: Selected Essays* (1984). Other works include the autobiographical works *Unmeisterliche Wanderjahre* (1971) and *Ortlichkeiten* (1980), *Hand an sich legen: Diskurs uber den Freitod* (on suicide) (1983), and several works on jazz.

In his introduction to *At the Mind's Limits,* Amery tells us that he has given much thought both to his reasons for writing this volume and to his audience. His writings about the Holocaust give us little information about his day-to-day life in the camps, but offer a powerful philosophical critique of what the Holocaust has meant for him and for society. In 1966 he addresses his audience:

> I do not address myself in this book to my comrades in fate. They know what it is all about. . . . To the Germans, however, who in their over-whelming majority do not, or no longer, feel affected by the darkest and at the same time most characteristic deeds of the Third Reich, I would like to relate a few things here that until now have perhaps not been revealed to them. Finally, I sometimes hope that this study has met its aims; then it could concern all those who wish to live together as fellow human beings. (p. xxiv)

In the early pages and preface to the second edition of his book, Amery continues:

> It is my concern that the youth of Germany—the ones who are flexible, intrinsically liberal and striving for Utopia, that is, the young people of the Left—do not slip over unawares to those who are their enemies as well as mine. . . . Let this book then. . . . be a witness not only to what *real* Fascism and *singular Nazism* were, but let it also be an appeal to German youth for introspection . . . since I neither can nor want to get rid of [my resentments], I must live with them and am obliged to clarify them for those against whom they are directed. (pp. xix, xx, 67)

He describes his work as "a personal confession refracted through meditation. . . . an examination or, if you will, a phenomenological description of the existence of the victim" (p. xix).

Charlotte Delbo (1913–1985)

Charlotte Delbo's trilogy *Auschwitz and Beyond* (1995)[4] is poetically and ironically beautiful. I identified closely with her interest in literature and the written word, her non-Jewishness, her splitting in two: an honest despair and a daily life of friends, work, and words that dance around the despair of honest memory. As with Amery's essays, there is little direct autobiographical here.

Delbo was a non-Jewish member of the French resistance, imprisoned in Auschwitz in January 1943. When France fell to the Nazis in June 1940, Delbo had been in Brazil as secretary to Louis Jouvet's theater company. She returned to France in 1941 and joined the Resistance. On March 2, 1942, the French police arrested her, along with her husband, resistance leader Georges Dudach. The French handed Dudach over to the Gestapo, who shot him to death in prison at Mont-Valerien on May 23, 1942.

The Gestapo imprisoned Delbo at La Lante and Fort de Romainville, and sent her to Auschwitz in January 1943. She writes of arriving at Auschwitz:

> But there is a station where those who arrive are those who are leaving
>
> a station where those who arrive have never arrived, where those who have left never came back.
>
> It is the largest station in the world.
>
> this is the station they reach, from wherever they came.
>
> They get here after days and nights
>
> having crossed many countries
>
> they reach it together with their children, even the little ones who were not to be part of this journey.
>
> They took the children because for this kind of trip you do not leave without them.
>
> those who had some took gold because they believed gold
>
> might come in handy.
>
> All of them took what they loved most because you do not leave your dearest possessions when
>
> you set out for far-distant lands.
>
> Each one brought his life along, since what you must take with you, above all, is your life.

> *And when they have gotten there they think they've arrived in*
> *Hell maybe. And yet they did not believe in it.*
>
> *They had no idea you could take a train to Hell but since they*
> *were there they took their courage in their hands ready to*
> *face what's coming. . . . They do not know there is no arriving*
> *in this station. they expect the worst—not the unthinkable.*
> *(pp. 3-4)*

In January 1944 she was sent to Ravensbruck. Shortly before the end of the war, the Red Cross arranged for her release to Sweden. After liberation, Delbo was a leading intellectual and writer in Paris until her death from cancer on May 1, 1985, but she has remained less well known in the United States. She wrote her story of Auschwitz immediately after her liberation, but waited twenty years to have it published. As she explained to Rosette Lamont, "I wanted to make sure it would withstand the test of time, since it had to travel far into the future" (1990, p. x).

Until 1995, *None of Us Will Return* (1965) was the only part of Delbo's Auschwitz trilogy that had been published in English. That volume had been translated into English in 1965. A new translation (by Rosette Lamont) of her entire Auschwitz trilogy, *Aucum de nous ne Reviendra* (None of Us Will Return), *Une Connaissance Inutile* (Useless Knowledge), and *Mesure de nos Jours* (The Measure of Our Days) was published by Yale University Press in 1995, and entitled *Auschwitz and After*. In 1990 Rosette C. Lamont's translation of *La Memoire et les Jours*, was published by Marlboro Press as *Days and Memory*. A 1997 collection of her writings, *Convoy to Auschwitz: Women of the French Resistance,* is included in a Northwestern University Press series, "Women's Life Writings From Around the World." Delbo's plays include "Que rapportera ces paroles?" (1966) first performed in 1974, and translated in English as "Who Will Carry the Word?" (1982), and several untranslated from the French. Delbo's translator tells us that Delbo repeatedly spoke of her writing as one way of ensuring that "such a horror would not happen again" (Lamont 1990, p. viii).

Fania Fenelon (1918–1983)

Fania Fenelon's story of being a musician at Auschwitz, *The Musicians of Auschwitz* or *Playing for Time* (1977),[5] caught my attention as the first Auschwitz writing I encountered by—and not just about—a musician. I'd read disparaging accounts of these musicians in other writings, describing them variously as traitors, collaborators, and privileged persecutors. The musicians I knew were none of these things, and I wondered if Auschwitz could so distort what I'd known to be inspiring and life-enhancing. Only a very amateur clarinet player, I recognized the pressure for perfection, but not the literal life-and-death consequences of mistakes. I recognized the ideal of performance as gift, but not Fenelon's reality of performance as desecration. She writes as one who has been repeatedly violated, not as a collaborator. I felt something of the defilement she felt as I read of Nazis weeping to hear Fania sing their favorite arias, appropriating her music, voice, and being for their own purposes. Her performances confirmed their self-definitions as sensitive proponents of high culture, morally separate from their murderous selves.

Fenelon gives the outlines of her pre-camp musical career, but few other personal details. Much of what I know about her comes from newspapers, musical encyclopedias, and her preface. Fania Fenelon was born in Paris as Fanny Goldstein on September 2, 1918. Her father was Jewish and her mother Roman Catholic. Before the war she had studied music at the Conservatoire de Paris for seven years and performed widely as a pianist and soprano soloist. She joined the French Resistance in 1940 because, as she explained later in an interview with *New York Times* reporter Susan Heller Anderson:

> I saw Hitler standing on top of the Arc de Triomphe... It filled me with such loathing I swore I would spend my life doing what I could to destroy this plague. (1978, p. 42)

Being fluent in French, German, English, and Russian, she was a valuable asset to the Resistance. From 1940–1943 she worked for the Resistance, using her talents for performance to gain access to German documents:

> I sang in cabarets where German officers went. When they were drunk I would photograph the contents of their briefcases and pass the film along. (1978, p. 42)

This work led to her arrest in 1943, nine months of imprisonment and torture in the French detention house Drancy, and deportation to Auschwitz on January 23, 1944. At Auschwitz Fenelon had spent two days in a quarantine bloc, when someone recognized her from her role in "Madame Butterfly." She successfully "auditioned" for a position as a soloist for the camp orchestra—accompanied on a Bechstein grand piano—and remained with the orchestra as vocal soloist, composer, and pianist. As Fenelon described it, part of the orchestra for which she wrote music was made up of "several violinists and guitarists, pipes, an accordion and . . . percussion" (p. 45). Her position offered some protection: daily showers, heat, individual beds, clean clothes, and indoor work—but no increase in food rations.

Fenelon frequently sang for the SS, including Maria Mandel, the Lagenfuhreren or chief of the women's camp. Mandel's first request of Fenelon is for a 3:00 a.m. performance of *Madame Butterfly*. Fenelon obeys, her voice a disembodied instrument:

> Mandel had removed her cape and sat down, looking dreamy. Could it be that she regarded herself as a sentimental geisha? I hated myself at the thought of giving her pleasure.
>
> But was I? Her face wasn't smiling, or even relaxed. Later, I was to learn that it was the done thing for the SS to listen to us as if we were slot machines. (p. 62)

Fenelon remained in Auschwitz until November 1, 1944, when she and the entire women's orchestra were force-marched to Bergen-Belsen. At the concentration camp at Bergen-Belsen, there was neither orchestra nor special privileges. Fenelon became ill with typhus. Near death, she was liberated by the British on April 15, 1945 (Anderson, 1978).

On May 17, 1945, Fenelon returned to Paris and joined a troupe entertaining G.I.'s from the States. She soon moved to East Germany, where she was professor of music at conservatories in Dresden, Leipzig, and East Berlin. Some thirty years after liberation, Fenelon wrote down her memories of the women's orchestra at Auschwitz, translated as *The Musicians of Auschwitz* (1977) or *Playing for Time* (1976, 1977). She retired and returned to Paris in 1972, where she died of cancer on December 17, 1983. At the time of her death, she had begun a second book on the Holocaust, which she described in 1978 as being on "reinsertion into society" (1978, p. 43). She had promised her friends of the orchestra that she would write "this book about our orchestra" (1977, p. viii). Her writing, she tells us thirty years after liberation, is an attempt to "exorcise the orchestra" (1977, p. ix).

Szymon Laks (1901–1983)

I was first drawn to Szymon Laks' *Music of Another World* (1989)[6] as a contrast to Fania Fenelon's account of music at Auschwitz. A first-person account by a prominent Jewish member of the men's orchestra at Auschwitz, it seemed a perfect foil, a tool for exploring gendered differences between survivors. But as with all the books I chose, it is much more complex and compelling on its own merit. While the contrasts between the stories of the two musicians are obvious, I also found myself admiring Laks' efforts to maintain remnants of his personal identity even when greatly challenged, as well as his self-critical honesty.

Szymon Laks was born in Warsaw on November 1, 1901, to an assimilated Jewish family. Before the war he had studied math at the Vilnius University from 1919–1921, music at the Warsaw conservatory from 1921–1924, and music at the Paris Conservatory in 1926. He then was employed as a composer in Paris until his arrest by the Germans in 1941. In contrast to the other survivors, he pointedly omits the details of his arrest, telling us:

> I will not describe the circumstances in which I was arrested or the conditions in which my "resettlement" by the occupier took place. The only reality of this seventy-two-hour trip [to Auschwitz] was the unimaginable crush of deportees in cattle cars and the hallucinations caused by an impossible-to-satisfy thirst. (p. 20)

Of his arrival at Auschwitz, he remembers only fragments:

> So far I have not been able to recreate this moment, though I have tried very hard. Perhaps it is a question of memory, which fades; recollections, which deceive. In any case, as far as I am concerned, the slender fragments of memory make up a hazy impression, as though this collision with camp life had plunged me into a lethargic stupor and at the same time as though I had been shot from a catapult to another planet. One thing I remember

perfectly: the first questions I asked myself were, What kind of a world is this? What sort of creatures are those zebralike beings with shaved heads, some athletic, stout, others infirm, swaying on their feet, emaciated like skeletons?

I tried to shake off this nightmare, to tell myself that it was a dream, but an awakening did not come. What did come, though, was a swift, abrupt answer to all questions.

I no longer had a first and last name. I had become a number. My identity was number 49,543 tattooed on my left forearm for the rest of my life. (p. 20)

Laks remained at Auschwitz for two and a half years, from July 1942 through November 1944, as violinist and conductor of the men's orchestra. In November 1944, he was evacuated from Auschwitz to Dachau's subcamp Kauferings. Kauferings was abandoned by the German guards on April 29, 1945, and liberated by the Americans on May 3, 1945. After liberation, and until his death in 1983, Laks worked as a composer in Paris among Polish Jewish expatriates, where he worked to promote national music within Polish emigre circles. Many of his compositions are based on Polish folk music and Jewish musical themes. Major international musical encyclopedia, such at the *International Cyclopedia of Music and Musicians* (Bophle 1975) and *The New Grove Dictionary of Music and Musicians* (Sadie 1980), cite his works.

Laks wrote his story in French in 1948 and included in it an adaptation of "Three Warsaw Polonaises" that he had written while at Auschwitz. In the 1950s the Polish government rejected the Polish translation of his manuscript for its "overly favorable" (Laks 1989, p. 3) depiction of the Germans. Laks revised the manuscript shortly before his death, and it was translated into English in 1989. Excerpts from his writing were published by the *Washington Post* as "Orchestra of the Doomed" in 1990. He described his original writing as "a small book, in French, about the orchestra that had existed in the camp and about the kinds of music that had been played there" (p. 3) and tells of an ethical imperative to tell this story:

> Since for a long time I was a member of the orchestra in Auschwitz II and during a certain period its conductor, I regard it as my obligation to relate and in some way to commemorate

this strange chapter in the history of music, a chapter that will probably not be written by any professional historian of this branch of art. (p. 6)

Laks lived the remainder of his life in Paris, active within a circle of Polish emigres as a promoter of Polish music. His compositions include several orchestral works, chamber pieces, and numerous Polish songs. He is also the author of a 1976 Polish publication titled "Epizody, Epigramy, Epistoly," in which he gives his memories of the painter Tadeusz Makowski. Laks died in Paris in 1983.

Primo Levi (1919–1987)

I was familiar with some of Primo Levi's writing before reading his stories of Auschwitz. I'd read his *Periodic Table* (1984) and found him a witty yet sensitive writer. I felt myself drawn to an image I had of him as a dignified, humble, honest, and brilliant man. His Auschwitz writings reinforced—and complicated—this image. Levi struck me as extremely honest about the role "luck" played in survival and the moral complexities of Auschwitz, but he was reticent in revealing the details of his life. I identified with his theological skepticism, and his intellectual distance resonated with my own writing preferences.

Levi was born in his family home in Turin, in the Piedmont region of Italy, where his family had lived for generations. Although his family did not practice Judaism, he was well read in Jewish and secular literature. In 1939 he earned a doctorate in chemistry, and began work as a chemist. In 1943 Levi, along with several university friends, joined the poorly equipped anti-Fascist Partisan Resistance Movement, "Justice and Liberty," in the Italian mountains. On December 13, 1943, Italian fascists attacked the group, killing several and arresting Levi. In the following passage he tells how he—perhaps mistakenly—felt safer in his Jewish identity than in his partisan identity:

> During the interrogations that followed [my arrest by the Fascist militia] I preferred to admit my status of "Italian citizen of Jewish race." I felt that otherwise I would be unable to justify my presence in places too secluded even for an evacuee; while I believed (wrongly as was subsequently seen) that the admission of my political

> activity would have meant torture and certain death. As a Jew I
> was sent to Fossoli, near Modena, where a vast detention camp,
> originally meant for English and American prisoners-of-war, col-
> lected all the numerous categories of people not approved of by
> the non-born Fascist Republic. . . . On the morning of the 21st [of
> February] we learned that on the following day the Jews would be
> leaving. . . . Our destination? Nobody knew. (1961, p. 10)

This unknown destination was Auschwitz. Levi remained there
from February 1944 until January 27, 1945. There he was assigned
a variety of manual labor jobs, and eventually worked as a chemist at the Buna rubber plant.

Following the war, Levi returned to Turin and worked there
as a chemist at a paint factory. He wrote *Se questo un uomo* immediately upon return home. It was published in Italian in 1947, and
first translated as *If This Is a Man* (1959). The book is now available
as *Survival in Auschwitz: The Nazi Assault on Humanity* (1961, 1996).
A decade and a half later, he wrote a sequel, published in Italian
as *La Tregua*, The Truce (1963), and in English as *The Reawakening*
(1965). In *The Reawakening* Levi tells of his eight-month journey
home from Auschwitz through Poland, Ukraine, and Belorussia
to Turin. Levi retired in 1974 to devote himself full-time to writing.
His other best known publications available include two collec-
tions of essays, *The Periodic Table* (1975, 1984) and *Other People's
Trades* (1989), and a series of Auschwitz-based stories, *Moments of
Reprieve* (1981, 1986), and *The Drowned and the Saved* (1986, 1988).

At the end of the war, Levi's family home was untouched and
his entire family was alive. He lived there until his death on April
11, 1987, following a fall down a stairwell in his family home—
presumably a suicide.

Sara Nomberg-Przytyk (1915–1990?)

While I was a doctoral student at Western Michigan University, my advisor began including Sara Nomberg-Przytyk's *True
Tales from a Grotesque Land* (1985a) in the Holocaust class he
teaches. Students responded very positively to this book. Her
stories address uniquely female concerns of Auschwitz prisoners
such as pregnancy, childbirth, and menstruation not included in
the course's male-authored readings. For them and for me,

Nomberg-Przytyk's words, with their emphasis on daily life in Auschwitz, helped bridge the chasm between survivors' lives and ours, and powerfully reminded us of the individuality of survivors and victims alike.

Nomberg-Przytyk was born in Lublin, Poland, to a poor Hasidic family. Her grandfather was a Rabbi, a well-known Talmudist, the principal at the Yeshiva in Warsaw. She was a student at the university in Warsaw and active in the Communist Party. In the 1930s Nomberg-Przytyk spent five years as a political prisoner, and from 1941–1943 she was confined to the Bialystok Ghetto. From Bialystok, she was deported to Stutthoff. After two months in Stutthoff, Nomberg-Przytyk and the other Jewish prisoners were ordered to change from their filthy camp uniforms and board a train:

> For the trip we were give winter uniforms and the commandant was inspecting them to make sure that there were no holes and that all the buttons were sewed on. . . . the SS man turned to us and politely told us to board the train. . . . a second guard came in with food. Everybody was given a slice of bread, a piece of margarine, and a piece of cheese . . . [Each morning] more food was brought in, accompanied by a large thermos of hot coffee and a few cups . . . [and each day] we received a full day's ration of food: bread, margarine, cheese, and red sausage. The curtains were drawn across the window, and the SS man did not allow them to be opened. (pp. 9–11)

One evening the prisoners arrive at their destination:

> At that moment the devil in our escorts showed himself. "*Raus, raus schneller*" (Out, out, faster") they shouted, smashing us across our heads with their rifles. . . . We had reached the border, all right, the border of Hell. (p. 12)

Nomberg-Przytyk remained at Auschwitz from January 13, 1944–January 18, 1945, where her communist colleagues found her a job as a receptionist in the camp infirmary. Although she worked in the infirmary's reception area, Nomberg-Przytyk was listed as a patient at the infirmary, and was thus able to eat and sleep there. Shortly before liberation, she was evacuated from Auschwitz to Ravensbruck, then to Rostock. In April 1945, Rostock was liberated by Russian, British, and American armies.

After the war Nomberg-Przytyk returned to Poland where she worked as a journalist in Lublin for over two decades. In 1968 Nomberg-Przytyk and her two sons moved to Israel. *Auschwitz: True Tales from a Grotesque Land*, written in Polish in 1966, had been accepted for publication in Poland, but the Polish government canceled the contract subsequent to the Six-Day War in 1972. She left her Auschwitz writings in the archives at Yad Vashem, and emigrated to Canada in 1975. Eli Pfefferkorn discovered her memoirs at Yad Vashem, and Roslyn Hirsch began translating them into English in 1981. They were published for the first time—in English—in 1985. Nomberg-Przytyk lived in Canada with her son until 1990 when she died of complications of polio. Her other publications include *Pillars of Samson* (1966) and *Esther's First Born* (1985b), an excerpt from *Auschwitz: True Tales from a Grotesque Land.*

All six memoirists tell of events of the same time (from mid-1943 to mid-1945) and place (the few hundred acres that comprised Auschwitz). Today this place is a museum, a monument, a vast graveyard, and a site of pilgrimage for over half a million people annually. Maps and signs refer to the surrounding towns as Oswiecim and Brezinka, and to the camp by its German names, Auschwitz and Birkenau.

AUSCHWITZ

The town of Oswiecim was part of the Hapsburg Empire from 1772 through 1918, and was central to the establishment of the independent Polish republic. In 1939, the population of Oswiecim was around 12,000, of which almost 5,000 were Jews. The Germans renamed this Polish district town Auschwitz in 1939. By 1944, Auschwitz had become the largest and most complex of the Nazi camps, an extermination camp, and a work camp.

Over the past few years I have heard several speakers talk about the physical structure of the Auschwitz Concentration Camp System. Robert Jan van Pelt, an architect and historian, speaks and writes in great detail about the historical role the architectural plans for Auschwitz played in the Holocaust. He tells us that the Germans, in particular Heinrich Himmler, deemed it an ideal site for massive resettlement of ethnic Germans, a model medieval-style farming village, calling it "a paradigm of the settlement in the East" (1994, p. 106). To clear the site for ethnic Germans, Himmler decreed that all Poles and Jews would be removed from the area.

Located at the intersections of the Sola, Przemsa, and Vistula rivers, near a gravel and sand production facility acquired by the DEST (German Earth and Stone Works), and only 50 kilometers southwest of Krakow, Oswiecim was deemed an ideal spot for industry as well. Thus the I.G. Farbin Company decided to locate there in 1941 and construction began on the plant and workers' barracks. Within a couple of years, the camp took on new functions. It became a forced labor camp, a transit site, a prison for Polish Resisters, an execution site, and finally, a site of mass murder.[7]

Since most Jews were gassed when they arrived at Auschwitz, the exact number of victims is not known. Only 404,222 people were registered at Auschwitz with tattoo numbers. Rudolf Hoess, Commandant at Auschwitz from 1940–1945, claimed in his 1947 memoir that 2.5 million were killed at Auschwitz. Current estimates of those killed range from one to four million, with best estimates at 1.3 to 1.6 million. On some days in 1944, as many as 20,000 individuals were, in the words of the murderers, "processed." A pamphlet that I purchased at the Auschwitz Museum on July 10, 1996, reads:

> [O]ut of a total of 1,300,000 people deported to Auschwitz-Birkenau over the period from 1940 to 1945, at least 1,100,000 perished in the camp. These two figures must be regarded as minimum estimates based on balance-sheets of numbers of deportees from various countries and decreases in the size of the camp's prisoner population. (Piper 1994, p. 49)

Only about 65,000 prisoners survived Auschwitz, less than one percent of all who were sent there.

Today Auschwitz remains the site of contested memories, stories, and histories.[8] The commemorative tablets at Birkenau have been recently rewritten to reflect changes in estimates of victims, and the acknowledgment that most of the murdered were Jewish. The original message inscribed in 1967 in twenty languages, on twenty stone tablets, read, "Four million people suffered and died here at the hands of the Nazi murderers between the years 1940 and 1945." Twenty-three years later, the new Polish government removed the words from the tablets. When I visited the camp in November 1993, the tablets were still blank. In July 1996, the tablets—again in twenty languages, including English, Hebrew, Yiddish, Polish and German—read:

> FOR EVER LET THIS PLACE BE
> A CRY OF DESPAIR
> AND A WARNING TO HUMANITY,
> WHERE THE NAZIS MURDERED
> ABOUT ONE AND A HALF
> MILLION
> MEN, WOMEN AND CHILDREN,
> MAINLY JEWS
> FROM VARIOUS COUNTRIES OF EUROPE.
> AUSCHWITZ-BIRKENAU
> 1940–1945

Much of the debate over numbers centers on questions of allowable evidence. Documentary or administrative evidence points to higher numbers, while forensic evidence "includes only those for whom traces of established evidence remain" (Adam 1989, p. 151). Using forensic evidence, Adam estimates that the Nazis murdered about 1,334,700 people at Auschwitz, including 1,323,000 Jews and 6,430 Gypsies (Adam 1989, p. 354, n. 108). At the time of liberation, only 7,600 prisoners remained alive at Auschwitz. Approximately 66,000 (Krakowski 1990) to 68,000 (Buszko 1990) others had been forcibly marched toward Germany. Of these, at least 15,000 died en route to the west.[9]

At some level, debates about numbers murdered are offensive. Not knowing to the nearest tenth of a million how many were slain underscores the extent to which individual lives had lost all meaning to the machinery that literally consumed them. It also suggests that the magnitude of the offense can be precisely calculated: that the greater the number killed the greater the offense.

MEMORY AND STORY

For Hannah Arendt storytelling is central to all scholarly endeavor (1978). She reminds me that I live, think, and write within webs of others' stories.[10] Even when I write as a theorist, I am a storyteller, culling from existing stories and constructing new tellings. These survivors are also story-tellers, choosing which events to narrate, which to omit. As Hutcheon reminds us, what is written is never identical to the event about which it is written, for the "facts of history" tell their stories through textualized traces.

The Durkheimian tradition of collective knowledge and representations has much to say to me about how survivors tell their stories, and even more about how I read them.[11] It reminds me that I know of events in the world—including in the lives of Auschwitz survivors—indirectly, through stories or representations of the events. The very categories of understanding by which we organize knowledge are socially constructed (Durkheim 1965; Mestrovic 1988). Survivors write—and I read—from within webs of time, space, and others' lives. I thus approach, read, and reflect upon these stories with the premise that "the world can never be known as a thing-in-itself; reality can never speak for itself" (Reissman 1993, p. 2).

The results have been an evolving and inseparable reading and re-reading of both forms of story. My writing, as simultaneously story and theory, is interwoven with and sustained by a rich and diverse fabric of others' stories. The major strands of this story come from the voices of survivors themselves. The entire tapestry is framed and supported by feminist readings of collective memory and life writing. I have woven into the fabric of my story quotes from others whose specific words anchor my reflections.

Feminist thinking on life stories and writing also guides my reading. Bakhtin's writings offer support for honoring the multiple voices of both women and men. Feminists such as Dale Bauer and S. Jaret McKinstry (1991), Sheryl Stevenson (1991), Diane Price Herndl (1991), and Clair Wills (1989) draw from Bakhtin to argue for multiple readings or interpretations of any story.[12] Their works reinforced the path my readings have taken.

I approach these stories with two paradoxical assumptions. On the one hand stories of Auschwitz make the events of Auschwitz more accessible to me than other forms of telling. Giving events narrative structure helps us make sense of our worlds and our experiences and "wards off chaos" (Griswold 1994, p. 20). We hang the events of our lives upon narrative structures and turn them into stories. We select and arrange fragments into orderly sequences, telling our stories as if they had inherent beginnings, middles, and endings, as if cause and effect has been operative and visible (Bladick 1990; Langer 1991, p. 203; McCabe 1991, p. ix; Miller 1991, p. 67).[13] Thus our stories, and the ones we hear and read, achieve an authority as they resonate with our own desires for understanding and significance.

On the other hand, narrative structure also keeps me, as both reader and writer, from directly encountering these same events. To read stories such as Elie Wiesel's as representative and universal is to, in part, misread. All re-tellings are assembled from bits of lived experiences and memories (Culler 1982; Robbins 1992; Prince 1992). Paying attention to narrative structure draws attention to processes by which survivors order and organize the events of their memories into coherent wholes. Structural form alters the content of what is communicated, making narrative structure central to communication, and removes me as reader from the actual events being narrated. Thus processes, forms, and modes of emplotment are inherently intertwined with interpretation, meaning, and form. Experienced events, in particular those of chaos, do not fit neatly into narrative structure—they must be "tidied up" and organized to form cohesive wholes (McCabe 1991, p. xi; White 1987).

An awareness of narrative structures and processes also helps me recognize the particularity and limited perspectives of all personal stories. Survivors often tell us that they experienced Auschwitz as pandemonium, and that their stories are merely sequenced remnants of memory. Eva Kor (1992), Auschwitz survivor and a subject of Mengele's twins experiments, reminds us that she and other prisoners were not "briefed" on research designs and protocols at Auschwitz.

Arthur W. Frank's writings (1995) on narratives of suffering speak to the frameworks that anchor my thoughts and readings.[14] Frank describes three general motifs common to tales of suffering–restitution, quest, and chaos. Within reassuring "restitution" narratives, individuals suffer greatly, experience great loss, but are restored to health and losses are replaced. These stories demonstrate a level of ultimate justice in which the innocent do not suffer without compensation, and only evil is punished. In spite of its emotional and ethical appeal, I believe that this framework has limited relevance for much of the reality of suffering of the twentieth century: those murdered can be neither restored to life nor replaced.

Quest narratives offer an alternative style of closure, in which what has been lost remains lost, but the hero overcomes or rises above challenges. Three stages characterize the quest narrative–departure from society, initiation into suffering, and return to society. The return is accompanied by insights or wisdom for the betterment of the society. Quest narratives do not seek to deny horrors and chaos, but aspire to offer wisdom or at least prevent a reoccurrence of the Holocaust. My own story often follows this path, taking me on a quest for understanding and moral knowledge. Along the way there are temptations to offer false reassurance, believe good overcomes evil, and run to an imaginary place where the stories of Auschwitz cannot affect my own.

Chaos narratives, to which I draw attention in Chapter Five, are actually "anti-narratives," stories lived rather than told. They reach beyond time, sequence, reflection, and meditation, and beyond the capacities of story-telling. They are the lived experiences that can be told around, but never told in, their essence. In contrast to restitution and quest narratives, chaos narratives are difficult to hear. They offer no reassurance of happy endings, no lessons to be learned, no models for rising above evil and suffering. They threaten the listener by exposing suffering beyond the grasp of language and redemption. But truth demands that we also listen for chaos stories of Auschwitz. We must remember that "the antidote to this pretense of invulnerability [found in restitution and quest stories] is chaos stories, reminding us that some situations cannot be risen above" (Frank 1995, p. 135).

Paying close attention to personal narratives draws attention to the stories peripheral to the grand narratives of history. While so-called representative biographies have been seen as windows to the dynamics of an age, a plurality of personal stories—often in the first person—illustrates the general with the particular.[15] While survivors' words point to the events of Auschwitz, they also remind us that individuals lived and died there, together and alone.

In thinking of a single story of grand narrative, I include not only those stories of an individual person universalized to all of a particular category, but also any universalized story. One form of grand narrative is the composite story, deliberately pieced together from fragmented testimony into one story. In such a narrative, to borrow the words of Sidonie Smith and Julia Watson, particular stories

> . . . can be read collectively as one story refracted through multiple lives, lives that share a common experience. (1992, p. 4)

Thus some story-tellers have encapsulated all survivors' tales by creating from fragmented testimony one grand narrative, one authoritative story that subsumes the particular into the universal, and serves as a standard for legitimating other stories. Des Pres, for example, examined a wide range of Holocaust testimony, and attempted "to provide a medium through which these scattered voices [of Holocaust survivors] might issue in one statement" (1976, p. vi). The very title of his book, using the singular *Survivor*, reflects his attempt to conflate particular diverse stories into one seamless universal story. He has chosen what he deems typical events and pieced them together. As if piecing together a quilt, he has stitched scraps of life and death together into a whole. As human documents, testimonies differ from historical accounts of the Holocaust. The word "testimony" asks that I read not to search for a grand theory or concept of truth, but to listen for individual, situated, and irreplaceable stories.

My challenge to grand narratives does not imply that all stories are meaningless, but the antithesis, that the individual story is full of meaning and worth, and need not–should not–match or be subsumed by grand narratives. Stories of survivors and victims alike work against subsumption and the disappearance of the individual. My purpose is not to challenge the authenticity of this literature, but to emphasize the individuality of lived experiences.

SILENCE AND VOICE

The "Final Solution"–to use the perpetrators' phrase–decreed that there would be no survivors, no witnesses to tell their stories, no one to write their stories of imprisonment in Auschwitz. In the stories of the survivors, one particularly cruel form of harassment was the taunt by guards and the SS that even if they survived, no one would believe their words. Laks tells of such an incident in which a Nazi officer sums up the prevailing judgment of the camp:

> "You see, . . . according to the instructions of the Fuhrer him-self, not even one *Haftling* [prisoner] should come out alive from any concentration camp. In other words, there will be no one who can tell the world what has happened here in the last few years. But even if such witnesses should be found–and this is the essence of the brilliant plan of our Fuhrer–NOBODY WILL BELIEVE THEM. . . . Even if we lose the war . . . no one will present us with the reckoning." (p. 79)

Survivors' stories come from the margins of history and tell of individuals marked for death as "Other." Spoken with voices that the machinery of Auschwitz intended to forever silence, all survivors' voices–female and male–defy annihilation.[16]

I am not the first to struggle with issues of putting the Holo-caust into words. In the wake of Auschwitz, there has been a long history of debates on silence, testimony, and voice. In the words of the Holocaust literary critic Lawrence Langer, I ask, "how should art–how can art?–represent the inexpressibly inhuman suffering of the victims, without doing an injustice to that suffering? . . . [Isn't there] something disagreeable, almost dishonorable, in the conversion of the suffering of the victims into works of art?" (1975, p. 1)

Themes of silence and bearing witness operate in tension in many Holocaust writings. George Steiner titled his collected essays, *Language and Silence* (1967); David Patterson chose as the title for his 1992 book on the Holocaust, *The Shriek of Silence*. Claude Lanzmann filled his epic film *Shoah* (1985) with long and powerful silences, and wrote in response to Spielberg's film *Schindler's List*, "I deeply believe there are some things that cannot and should not be represented" (1994, p. 14). Linden describes "what Arendt referred to as 'sheer happenings'– fragments of experiences that refuse narrative forms–that literally cannot be talked about. 'Sheer happenings' are woven into Holocaust survivors' stories . . . as silences" (1993, p. 11) that cannot be legitimized into a common stock of knowledge.

Debates on silence about the Holocaust have become so commonplace–and even mandatory in Holocaust literature–that French philosopher Jean-Francois Lyotard, in *Heidegger and "the jews,"* suggests that to say, "Let's not talk about that" (1990, p. vii) has become a rhetorical device introducing discussion about the Holocaust. Total silence would be surrender and cynicism at best, a complicity in suppressing the victims' stories. Theodor Adorno, philosopher of the Frankfurt School, recognized that to be human in the wake of Auschwitz demands a voice, since "perennial suffering has as much right to expression as a tortured man has to scream, hence it may be wrong to say that after Auschwitz you could no longer write poems" (1973, p. 362). Novelist and essayist Cynthia Ozick's words speak for me when she writes of Auschwitz: "I cannot *not* write about it" (1988, p. 284).[17]

The words of Holocaust victims and survivors cannot and never will be dispassionate accounts of witnessed events. They are neither unmediated historical chronicles nor imagined fictions; neither mimetic representations nor ephemeral nightmares. They are, in part, stories, personal truths, and subjective presentations of self and others. Individually and collectively, they form a fragile bridge between incomprehension and awareness, between event and memory. They keep the Holocaust "within the bounds of history" (Howe 1988, p. 183). The words of Russian linguist Mikhail Bakhtin seem to me most fitting as I read and listen carefully:

> the understanding of the Fascist torture chamber or hell . . .
> [is an] absolute lack of being heard. . , . [T]he word . . . always wants

to be heard, always seeks responsive understanding. . . . For the word there is nothing more terrible than a lack of response. (1986, pp. 126, 127)

The survivors and the ghosts of their comrades call upon me, as reader and listener, to hear, to listen, to respond.

NOTES

1. See Appendix for a list of book-length Auschwitz memoirs published in English.

2. In his earlier writings, Holocaust literary scholar Lawrence Langer (1978) gives detailed analyses of Holocaust writing, including memoirs. He has, however, turned his attention to survivors' videotaped stories (1991), and now asserts that survivors' oral stories are more authentic because they cannot achieve narrative coherence and unity. They are more spontaneous and contain multiple and irreconcilable identities; they cannot be formed into a single life story. "The raw material of oral Holocaust narratives, in content and manner of presentation, resists the organizing impulse of moral theory and art" (1991, p. 204).

    I argue against privileging oral testimony over written stories. Instead, as feminist Holocaust scholar Joan Ringelheim (1985, 1990, 1993) points out, interviewees are in a unique position of being susceptible to trying to please a specific interviewer, and interviewers are susceptible to wanting to hear comfortable answers. All stories, whether written or oral, are discourse, and shaped by context and audience.

3. All quotes of Amery are from this volume unless otherwise indicated.

4. All quotes of Delbo are from this volume unless otherwise indicated.

5. All quotes of Fenelon are from this volume unless otherwise indicated.

6. All quotes of Laks are from this volume unless otherwise indicated.

7. See Dwork and van Pelt's "Reclaiming Auschwitz" (1994), van Pelt's "A Site in Search of a Mission" (1994), and van Pelt and Dwork's *Auschwitz: 1270 to the Present* (1996) for an extended chronicle of the complex and often haphazard degeneration of German plans for Auschwitz-Birkenau: from Himmler's utopian dreams of resettlement to its nefarious use as a center for mass extermination.

8. Since the first post-Communist government gained power in Poland, conflicts over the meanings of Auschwitz as a historical site have become more noticeable (Charlesworth 1994; Elon 1993; Kurlansky 1994; Young 1993). In addition, the Carmelite convent established at Auschwitz in 1984 has been the locus of an international dispute over competing memories of the Polish Catholic and Jewish victims (Hausknecht 1990; Lewis 1991; Rittner and Roth 1993; Suchecky 1994).

9. The *Auschwitz Chronicle: 1939–1945* (Czech 1990), the *Encyclopedia of the Holocaust* (Buszko 1990), *Auschwitz: A History in Photographs* (United States Holocaust Memorial Museum Research Institute 1993), *Anatomy of the Auschwitz Death Camp* (Gutman and Berenbaum 1994), and *Auschwitz: 1270 to the Present* (1996) are most helpful sources of historical details of Auschwitz.

10. As I reviewed the literature on stories, autobiography and plurality, I frequently came across references to the works of Hannah Arendt. Seyla Benhabib, for example, uses Arendt as a springboard for dialogue with Habermas, the Enlightenment, ethics, modernity, and postmodernity. Her discussion of Arendt is most helpful in her explorations of theorists as storytellers, plurality (1992, p. 138), and the webs of "narrative histories—both one's own and those of others" (1991, p. 129) in which all action and all interpretation is situated.

11. My sociological heritage has a long, if sporadic, practice of using personal narrative or life stories as sociological data. For exemplars of this tradition, see Dilthey (1961), Martineau (1853), Merton (1977), Mills (1959), and Thomas and Znaniecki (1918).

   Reclaiming Dilthey's late nineteenth-century work on biography as a topic and methodology for "Verstehen," a hermeneutics of biography has captured the imagination of sociologists who occupy the interdisciplinary realms where social science, literary and aesthetic criticism, and the humanities converge. Dilthey's work, of course, builds upon Weber's notion of "Verstehen" (1949) as a sociological method to come to know how people construct meaning in their lives.

   In the 1980s and 1990s there has been renewed interest in life stories among nonpositivistic sociologists working at the intersections of social sciences and the humanities. Much of this writing emerges from a convergence of qualitative and ethnographic methodologies, feminism and commitments to marginalized "Others." Examples include Denzin (1989a, 1989b, 1990, 1991, 1992), Ellis and Bochner (1996), Ellis and Flaherty 1992), Hill (1993) Linden (1993, 1996), Quinney (1996), Richardson (1994, 1996a, 1996b), and members of the British Auto/Biography group such as Erben (1993), Evans (1993), Stanley (1993), and Temple (1994).

12. Michael Gardiner, in one of the few sociological works on Bakhtin, writes incisively of Bakhtinian dialogics and ideology. He argues that while Bakhtin is frequently idealistic and even utopian, his critique of the monologism of the Enlightenment is a perceptive condemnation of European domination, "scientific rationalism, utilitarianism, and positivism" (1992, p. 169).

13. It was only in the late 1960s that the term "narratology" was coined to denote a particular branch of literary criticism "devoted to the analysis of narratives, and more specifically of forms of narration and varieties of narrator" (Bladick, p. 146). But the concept of narrative and its key components can be traced to Aristotle's *Poetics.* Aristotle delineated the

structure and processes of narrative: the unity of a structured linear plot, complication and unraveling or denouement, separated by a turning point. The plot may imitate action and order events to narrate a constructed unity of action. The described action may be "true to fact" but may also be the author's view of how the action ought to have been or how people have said that it is, a literal representation of events or action is not essential to poetic narrative (1956, pp. 9–36).

14. Thanks go to Carolyn Ellis and Arthur P. Bochner for introducing me to this work.

15. Mary Evans' proposed sociological use of personal narrative reflects a turn from inductive to deductive study of life stories, a "shift in the codes and subjects of biography" (1993, p. 8). Her work encourages me to perceive phenomena and events through stories of the less powerful.

16. Lesser known voices and the earlier stories of Wiesel and Levi are most obviously written from the margins. Levi's position within Holocaust canons has changed tremendously since the publication of his first book. His writings span thirty years and five books. A 1959 reading of Levi's first work *If This be a Man* is not the same as a 1984 reading of the same work, now translated as *Survival in Auschwitz*. In 1959 Levi was employed as a chemist, and his works were little known outside of his native Italy. But in 1984, his 1975 work *The Periodic Table* was translated into English, and his earlier works gained in popularity.

17. Ironically, those who speak most eloquently for silence in the wake of the Holocaust are seldom silent.

CHAPTER 2

Borrowed Memories
and Grand Narratives

Journal Entry: February 13–14, 1994

*I am in Washington, D.C. to visit the United States Holocaust
Memorial Museum. I spend Sunday, from 10 a.m. to 4 p.m. viewing
the permanent exhibit. Joan Ringelheim, Director of Oral History
at the museum, has left me a ticket so I do not have to stand in
long lines and jostle my way into the exhibit. I feel unjustifiably
privileged. Do survivors and their children also receive advance
tickets? Do they wait in endless lines to see and hear nationally
sanctioned stories of their pasts? My thoughts remind me of my
undeserved privilege and safety. I am one of those whom Lawrence
Langer calls "witnesses to memory rather than rememberers
themselves" (1991, p. 39).*

*While I wait, I reflect on the language by which we think of
these events of fifty years ago. Today we think of a historically
bounded phenomenon called the "Holocaust." A half-century
ago, there was no such understanding: there was murder, even
mass murder; there were fragments of experience, perception
and information; but there was no coherent story. For as "it"
happened, and even for years after, the phenomenon had no name.*

According to the *Encyclopedia of the Holocaust* (Gutman 1990), the term "Holocaust" comes from an ancient Greek word "holokauston," a sacrifice consumed by fire. In the Book of Samuel, it meant a burnt offering to God. Gradually, it came to mean large-scale human destruction. The Hebrew word for Holocaust, "sho'ah," was first used in 1940 to refer to the destruction of European Jews. Not until the 1950s did the term "Holocaust" become synonymous with the Nazi genocide of the Jews: in 1959 Ya'd Vashem began to use the term, and in 1968 the U.S. Library of Congress created a category called "Holocaust—Jewish, 1939–1945." In the genesis of this term, there is sociological—as well as etymological—significance. For until there is a word to describe a phenomenon, it does not exist in some cognitive sense. Before it was called Holocaust, it had no name; and it is difficult to conceptualize and remember—let alone pass on memories of—that which is not named.

It is time to begin. I join a crowd waiting to enter one of several elevators to the top floor, where the exhibit begins. There are two boxes of cards, one male and one female. A sign asks to take one (and only one, please) card, appropriate to one's sex. On the card is the story of one victim of the Holocaust. Some are also survivors. I do not follow orders. I take two cards, one from each box. Both are survivors.

In spite of icy roads and sidewalks, the museum is crowded. The tour is self-guided and aided by computer technology. Once one has gained admittance to the exhibit, it is all very efficient. The machinery of audio- and visual tapes and interactive computer programs runs very smoothly, processing an average of 4,200 visitors a day since its opening on April 26, 1993. A guard at the beginning of the exhibit announces that there are over nine hours of videotape in the permanent exhibit, and the museum is only open seven hours. I feel rushed and afraid. I imagine myself as part of an anonymous mass being herded into elevators and through the exhibitions.

I begin on the fourth floor, with an introduction and exhibits of pre-Holocaust worlds. The third floor covers the Holocaust itself, and the second looks at post-Holocaust life. Throughout, the United States plays roles of not-so-innocent bystander and victorious liberator. I see exhibits that the signs say are duplicates of what is at the Auschwitz I Museum. None look familiar. I pass through a box car and a section of barracks from Birkenau. I am especially interested in stories from the Netherlands and of women. The Dutch story tells me dates for the invasion of the Netherlands, survival statistics, and the story of Anne Frank. Women's voices are well represented in collages of audio- and videotaped survivors' stories. On an interactive computer I look up the names of the survivors I have been studying. I find the names of Elie Wiesel and Primo Levi, but none of the women.

Everywhere I turn I come face to face with individual stories, in photographs, audio-taped stories, video stories, in victim's remains: suitcases, glasses, and baby strollers. My children have asked me if the Nazis killed children. I've been truthful, but never before knew with my heart what this meant.

That night I dream that I am at Auschwitz with my sons, Alex and Arie. In the dream I know—but they do not—that they will soon be killed. I wake up trying to stop or delay their deaths, and refuse to go back to sleep for fear of the dream continuing. I lay awake for hours, crying for the mothers for whom Auschwitz was no mere nightmare, and for whom the suffering and deaths of their children was beyond endurance.

The next day I meet with two women on the staff of the Holocaust Museum's Research Institute, Joan Ringelheim and Sybil

Milton. We discuss our works-in-progress and the status of scholarship on gender and the Holocaust. I leave feeling that I have been given their blessings to pursue my writings, but eager to return home to reassure myself that my sons are still safe. I wonder if I am strong enough to continue this research. I cannot bear more dreams like last night's.

Journal Entry: December 11, 1994

I am reading a piece in *Ms.* by Andrea Dworkin entitled, "The Unremembered: Searching for Women at the Holocaust Memorial Museum" (1994). She critiques the museum for not providing an "explanation or narrative of [women's] persecution as *women* (p. 53), and concludes, "In the museum, the story of women is missing." (p. 54) Her attack strikes me as simplistic, essentialist, and separatist. I too, look for more stories, and more specific stories, of women during the Holocaust, but am less pessimistic about the museum's agenda. I did not feel excluded from the museum's stories, but was moved to tears and nightmares. These stories spoke to me of our common humanity, of individuals, families, and villages annihilated.

For many in the United States, this museum will be an introduction to the Holocaust. I think back to my first knowledge of the subject, one gleaned not from displays and videos, but from printed words of a girl frozen in death in 1945 at the age of 15.

Like many of my generation, my memories of the Holocaust are borrowed memories, formed through stories and images, words and pictures filtered through layers of telling and retelling. I took *Anne Frank: The Diary of a Young Girl* (1967) from my family's bookshelves when I was about the same age she was when she began writing it.

Anne Frank's diary has a richness that encourages multiple readings. For my father, her story spoke of the Europe he and his family left shortly before the war, relatives who joined the Dutch resistance, ethical questions about how he would have acted had he been faced with similar choices, and unanswerable questions of theodicy. My mother told me that the story evoked feelings of claustrophobic overcrowding, tensions of two households sharing living quarters, and constant fear of discovery. For Pete, my older brother, Anne Frank's diary told an adventure story.

For me, Anne Frank's story spoke of young people at the boundaries between childhood and adulthood, family conflicts, adolescent love, moodiness, and personal identity. Looking at my mother, born just a year before Frank, I wondered what lives Frank might have lived—had she been born in the United States, had she not been betrayed by a Dutch neighbor, had she not been Jewish. And with my own dark hair and eyes, I imagined that I looked like Anne Frank.

A few years later Elie Wiesel's Auschwitz story *Night* (1960) joined the shelves, and I borrowed it as well. I struggled with Wiesel as he mourned God's absence at Auschwitz. I did not, however, identify as closely with him as I did with Anne Frank. He spoke to me as an adult telling his life story to those of the next generation. I wept at his father's death, but felt safe in reassuring myself that these were stories of another time and place, carrying no intrinsic threat for me and my family. Wiesel's doubts about God's power and goodness haunted my father for the rest of his life, but it was not until I was an adult and faced the death of my own father that theological questions began to torment me.

These two stories dominated my borrowed memories of the Holocaust, and have certain parallels. Wiesel and Frank were born only one year apart, Wiesel in 1928 and Frank a year later. In 1944 both were sent by train with their families to Auschwitz, the largest and most complex of Nazi extermination and work camps. Both survived initial selections there, and lived for some months with a parent of the same sex. The parents with whom they lived at Auschwitz did not survive the Holocaust. Both Frank and Wiesel were taken from Auschwitz before liberation: Frank to Bergen-Belsen, and Wiesel to Buchenwald. Miraculously, some of each of their immediate families survived: Frank's father and Wiesel's sisters.

There are, however, important differences: most notably, Frank died shortly before liberation, while Wiesel survived. Although each tells a story of adolescence during the Holocaust, Frank wrote as an adolescent, and Wiesel wrote as an adult about himself as an adolescent. Frank's diary is taught more in secondary schools, and Wiesel's in colleges and universities. Frank's diary has a unique immediacy for young readers, and as Deborah Lipstadt notes, "for many readers it is their introduction to the Holocaust" (1993, p. 230). Today Wiesel speaks to us in the voice of a wise adult for whom the closure of "success" is assured to the reader at the beginning of the story. Frank's voice speaks as an adolescent, in the moment without knowledge of the outcome. In writing of Anne Frank and Elie Wiesel, I have often thought of them as a child and an adult, referring to them as "Anne" and "Wiesel." Frank remains in my thoughts a young girl forever fifteen years old.

Frank's work was published first in Dutch in 1947, and in English in 1952. It preceded Wiesel's original 1956 Yiddish publication by nine years and the 1960 English edition by eight. Frank's story was not only published earlier, but came to prominence much earlier than Wiesel's. By the mid-1950s Frank's work was so well known that Francois Mauriac, the Frenchman who had encouraged the young journalist Elie Wiesel to write his story, wrote in his foreword to *Night* that he hoped that the readers of Wiesel's story would become "as numerous as those of *The Diary of Anne Frank*" (1960, p. viii). Today his fame extends to his political activities, his role as a "messenger" from the Holocaust, and the many scholarly and popular articles and books he has written.

ANNE FRANK

Anne Frank's voice was heard in the United States as far back as the early 1950s and resonates through the decades. For many young American girls in the 1950s and 1960s, her voice was not only a voice from the Holocaust, but also a solitary voice speaking for us in a frightening world in which we often felt that our stories were unarticulated or ignored. "Anne Frank stood for all the Jews who were murdered in the Holocaust," according to Rose (1993, p. 76), "but she also stood for adolescent girls trying to assert their individuality in the complicated context of family life. Frank had written herself into being." In her diary I read a universal story of a young girl coming of age in the Netherlands, within the context of the Holocaust.

Anne Frank's story appeals to many others besides adolescent girls. For example, during a March 11, 1995, National Public Radio (NPR) discussion commemorating the fiftieth anniversary of Frank's death, NPR's Scott Simon interviewed Vincent Frank Steiner, President of the Anne Frank Foundation in Basel, Switzerland. Their words demonstrate the central role Frank's diary plays in shaping Holocaust memory and uses of her story in wider contexts:

> **Simon:** About 106,000 Dutch Jews were killed during . . . the Holocaust. . . .
>
> **Steiner:** But the only person which is known everywhere which has been killed in German Concentration Camps is Anna Frank [sic].
>
> **Simon:** Anne Frank's own true story, set down in her own words, has become the chronicle by which millions of people throughout the world are taught and reminded that hate kills. (p. 25)

I am not alone in my borrowed memories.

Frank's words, first published in Dutch as *Het Achterhuis* (The Room Behind the House) in 1947 and selling only fifteen hundred copies at that time, have long outlived her. Her diary was soon published in Germany and France (1950), and in England and the United States (1952). The 1955 play "The Diary of Anne Frank" won the Pulitzer Prize, the Critics' Circle Prize, and the Antoinette Perry Award, and was a featured Book Club selection in 1956 (Goodrich and Hackett 1956). It was made into a movie "The Diary of Anne Frank" (Stevens) in 1959, and re-released as a videocassette in 1997. In 1967 Meyer Levin privately published an alternative, but much less widely known play simply titled "Anne Frank." Today Frank's diary is available in over thirty languages in over fifty countries, and has sold more than twenty million copies.[1]

Anne Frank, author of only one major work, is linguistically inseparable from and conceptually linked to her diary. Other writings of hers, such as her short stories collected as *Anne Frank's*

Tales from the Secret Annex (1994) are now available in English, but with a reference to her diary and with her name and picture prominently displayed.

Anne Frank's story begins with an assimilated, well-to-do family in self-imposed exile in Amsterdam. She, her parents Edith and Otto Frank (code-named "Pim"), and her sister Margot fled there from Germany in 1933 to escape the Nazis. Anne Frank is bright, popular, and wealthy. Her world shrinks by degrees, until on July 6 of 1943 she and her family and the van Pels family (code-named the van Daans), including their son Peter, move into a cramped set of rooms called "het achterhuis" or "the annex" next to an office and storeroom where her father has worked. They are later joined by a dentist, Friedrich Pfeffer, code-named Albert Dussel. Anne Frank writes of family and friends, tensions and self-doubts, of thoughts and emotions (including a first love). On August 4, 1944, three days after Anne Frank's final entry in her diary, the Gestapo arrested the Frank family, the van Pels family, Fritz Pfeffer, and two Dutch people who had been helping them, Victor Kugler and Johannes Kleiman. Kugler and Kleiman were imprisoned in Amsterdam and survived the war. The eight who had been in hiding were sent to a prison in Amsterdam, then to Westerbork, a Dutch transit camp, and finally to Auschwitz. Of the eight in hiding, only Otto Frank survived the Holocaust. The ravages of war and the Holocaust are offstage, coming fully into play only after Anne Frank's last entry.

Anne Frank has not been the sole author of her work. The histories of her story, publication, production, and controversy point not only to her posthumous fame, but also to the lack of power, control and authority she has had over the fate of her story. Anne's father, Otto Frank, deleted much of what she wrote in her original diary as too private, too intimate, for public reading. His version of her diary (1947/1967) omits entire entries on her sexual anatomy (pp. 222, 234–234, 268), the arrest of a neighbor (pp. 212–213), and details of Otto's life (pp. 295–296). Each translation has edited and rewritten her words to make them palatable and acceptable. Each translation has conceded "alterations and suppression of material from the original diary." In many translations,

Anne Frank's story has been falsely universalized, with specifically Jewish aspects omitted or translated into more "neutral" terms (Rosenfeld 1991, p. 266).

Neither can Frank speak in her own defense to Holocaust deniers and critics such as psychologist and Holocaust survivor Bruno Bettelheim. Bettelheim (1960) wrote of her death, and that of her family, as a "natural consequence" of "foolish decisions" by the Franks to stay together and maintain a semblance of normality throughout their time of hiding. Such comments suggest a degree of agency completely inconsistent with the events. Holocaust deniers have seized upon Anne Frank's story in an attempt to discredit the best-known story of the Holocaust. It has been left to others, most notably the Netherlands State Institute for War Documentation (1989), to respond in word and in print to these accusations.

Anne Frank's story does not end with her own words. It has many endings, all written by others. In the late 1950s forty-two people who had known Anne Frank told her stories in a collection of interviews (Schnabel 1958). And more than forty years later, six women who had known Anne during the months between her last diary entry and her death told her stories through a Dutch television film documentary and a collection of their tales, *The Last Seven Months of Anne Frank*, now available in English (Lindwer 1988).

Initially, Frank did not intend her work for a public audience. Frank began her diary on June 12, 1942, addressing an imaginary friend. "I hope I will be able to confide everything to you, as I have never been able to confide in anyone, and I hope you will be a great source of comfort and support" (p. 1). Frank here follows the conventions of diary as a private "record of secret truth. . . . a place to relinquish control and to allow repressed material to surface . . . through a 'dialogue'" (Wiener and Rosenwald 1993, pp. 31, 42). In her second entry of Saturday, June 20, 1942, she wrote:

> I feel like writing, and I have an even greater need to get all kinds of things off my chest. . . . I'm not planning to let anyone else read this stiff-backed notebook grandly referred to as a "diary," unless I should ever find a real friend. . . Now I'm back to the point that prompted me to keep a diary in the first place: I

don't have a friend. . . . I want the diary to be my friend, and I'm
going to call my friend Kitty. (1995, pp. 6–7)[2]

It wasn't until March 29, 1944, that she wrote of having public
readers after the war. She wrote:

> Bolkestein, the Cabinet Minister, speaking on the Dutch broad-
> cast from London, said that after the war a collection would be
> made of diaries and letters dealing with the war. Of course every-
> one pounced on my diary. Just imagine how interesting it would
> be if I were to publish a novel about the Secret Annex. The title
> alone would make people think it was a detective story.
>
> Seriously, though, ten years after the war people would find
> it very amusing to read how we lived, what we ate, and what we
> talked about as Jews in hiding. (1995, pp. 243–44)[3]

Journal Entry: July 26, 1996

I have been studying the Netherlands National Exhibition at
Auschwitz for the past four weeks. I've taken pictures, measured
the exhibition, spoken with museum curators and visitors. This is
my last visit to the museum before returning to the States. I return
to the familiar portrait of Anne Frank. It is in a darkened section,
with a collection of photographs and documents about
Westerbork, here called a "Jewish transit camp," to which Anne
Frank and her family were sent before they were sent to Auschwitz.
The portrait is the one that I remember from the cover of her
published diary. The text to the left reads, "Westerbork was the
last wayside station for more than 100,000 Jews, one of whom was
Anne Frank." Anne Frank's portrait, one of six pictures on a larger
panel, is not prominent in this exhibition, measuring only about
eight by twelve inches.

Near the exit, in a large well-lighted room, I look again at the
picture of a girl, presumably Jewish, playing on a city street in the
Netherlands, that I remembered so well from my visit almost three
years ago. In contrast to the picture of Anne Frank, this one is many
times larger, reaching from the floor to the ceiling. It is paired with

a picture of the same size of the statue commemorating the dock workers' strike. I re-read and copy down the text between the two pictures. It reads, in Dutch, Polish and English:

> The monster had been defeated
> It had killed fifty million people
> Two hundred and forty thousand in the Netherlands.
> One hundred and five thousand of the hundred and forty thousand
> Dutch Jews.
> Sixty thousand of them in Auschwitz.
> The world mourned its dead.
> The world celebrated its liberation.
>
> The monster had lost.
> The Final Solution had failed.
> Six million Jews had been murdered.
> But the Jewish people had not been annihilated.
> There were survivors.
> In the Netherlands as elsewhere.
> The Netherlands again had a future.
> As had also its Jewish citizens.
>
> Even after those fearful years Jewish children still laugh and play.

Perpendicular to this picture, there is a copy of the statue represented in the picture. The statue, only about two feet tall, is the last item in the entire exhibition. Its text reads:

> 'The Dock Worker' by the sculptor Mari Andriessen, stands on the square which in February, 1941, was the scene of the first mass rounding up of Dutch Jews. It symbolizes the general protest strike which was the outraged response of their population of Amsterdam to this crime.

One visitor comments that the display suggests that the dock workers have resurrected Anne Frank. I think of the exhibition as a restitution narrative that places the Netherlands at its center. It is a story of a country that once lost many of its Jewish children, including Anne Frank, to a foreign monster. New children have succeeded those who died. If Anne Frank symbolizes the children who died in the Holocaust, this narrative ending tells us that her *story does not end with her words or even her death, but with the happy lives of those who have taken her place.*

I want to believe stories of Dutch tolerance and heroism, but I am sickened by the thought any person can take the place of a murdered child. I find in many Dutch stories of the Holocaust, stories of tolerance, rescue, and even self-criticism, a familiar self-righteousness which strikes too close to home.

Invented endings are even more striking in the staged version of Frank's diary. The play ends triumphantly with Frank's words, taken out of context from her diary, "In spite of everything, I still believe that people are good at heart." Such an ending seems calculated to insure that "audiences would leave the theater knowing, of course that Anne Frank had died but nevertheless feeling that she had not been defeated" (Rosenfeld 1991, p. 252). Frank had actually written these words in her diary on July 15, 1944, three weeks before being arrested by the Gestapo on August 4. In context, they give a less triumphal note:

> It's difficult in times like these: ideals, dreams and cherished hopes rise within us, only to be crushed by grim reality. It's a wonder I haven't abandoned all my ideals, they seem so absurd and impractical. Yet I cling to them because I still believe, in spite of everything, that people are really good at heart.
> It's utterly impossible for me to build my life on a foundation of chaos, suffering and death. I see the world being slowly transformed into a wilderness, I hear the approaching thunder that, one day, will destroy us too. (p. 332)

Anne Frank made her last diary entry on Tuesday, August 1, 1944. Her words reflect the soul-searching of an adolescent, the unbearable tension of hiding, and a growing knowledge that people are often anything but "good at heart." She wrote:

> A voice within me is sobbing. . . . I get cross, then sad, and finally end up turning my heart inside out, the bad part on the outside and the good part on the inside, and keep trying to find a way to become what I'd like to be and what I could be if . . . [sic] if only there were no other people in the world.
> Yours, Anne Frank. (p. 336)

It is unfaithful to Frank's story, and to the memory of all Holocaust victims, to suggest that her diary tells a universal story of good conquering evil, of hope in the midst of death.

ELIE WIESEL

Elie Wiesel's *Night* was the first well-known story of a Holocaust survivor. He tells us that he wrote his story for publication because, "I sensed clearly that the time had come to begin translating ten years of patient silence into words. . . . I felt an obligation to make my first book an offering to a culture, as atmosphere, a climate which were those of my childhood" (1987, p. 357). In 1956, long before he was well known, *Night* was first published in Yiddish under the title, *The World Was Silent.* Two years later an abridged version was published in French. In 1960, the French version was translated into English in the United States and given the current title of *Night.* The *Book Review Index* (beginning in 1965) shows relatively little attention paid to *Night* prior to Wiesel's 1986 Nobel Peace Prize, and increasing attention to *Night* and other works of his since. While his early works were not widely reviewed at the time of publication, *Night* is now almost uniformly included in bibliographies and syllabi on the Holocaust. *Night* has been translated into over eighteen languages. Repelled by trivialization and believing in the authentic power of words, Wiesel has refused to allow his story to be staged or filmed (Martelle 1992, p. 4–C).

Elie Wiesel's words capture much of the horror of the Jewish community, from ghetto to trains to camp, through selections, death, and, for a remnant, liberation. His story begins at about the same time as Anne Frank's, in a small Orthodox Jewish community in Hungary. He and his family are close and feel safe, in spite of deportation of foreign Jews and the warnings of one "Moshe" [Moses] who returned from Poland where he had been left for dead in a mass grave. Then Germany invades Hungary, and German troops occupy the town. Wiesel's family believes that the war will soon be over, and so they endure the arrests of Jewish leaders, confiscation of valuables, and a decree demanding that all Jews wear a yellow star.

Then comes a forced move to a crowded ghetto, establish-ment of a Jewish Council and police, and deportation of some, then all, ghetto residents by cattle wagons to an unknown desti-nation in the East. In the days and nights on the trains, countless individuals die of starvation, lack of water, and suffocation before they arrive at the platforms of Birkenau (Auschwitz II). On arrival there is the first selection: to the right for work, to the left for immediate death; it is a heinous game in which the players know neither the rules nor the consequences of their decisions. Families are torn apart and never see each other again. Those given a reprieve endure the degradations: stripped of all possessions, including clothing, and totally shaved, "disinfected," inspected, and given rags for clothing. What follows is a melange of confu-sion, unrelenting cruelty, senseless work, hunger, thirst, sickness, death, and finally, a march into Germany through days of snow, starvation, and bullets. Liberation comes only after most, including the rest of Wiesel's family, have died.

Journal Entry: October 23, 1994

I listen to Elie Wiesel speak to a gathering of Holocaust scholars at Dartmouth College. Security is tight. Only those of us attending the conference are allowed to sit in the front twenty rows. Before Wiesel speaks, he sits motionless on the stage with his head in his hands. He speaks deliberately, with passion, humility, and with a deep concern for the truths of each survivor's story. He speaks of truth and memory. For most of his talk, I forget any expectations I may have had. I am surprised to find myself in awe of this man. I better understand and respect his role as peace-maker and inspiration for overcoming evil. I feel that I am in the presence of greatness, not solely because Wiesel is a survivor, but because of his obvious love for and dedication to humanity.

Wiesel's story as written, spoken, and lived, evinces stories of all Holocaust survivors. He serves on Presidential Commissions, appears on late-night television, and wrote the foreword for the *Encyclopedia of the Holocaust.* His early work *Night* appears in most college and university course syllabi on the Holocaust, and is the most widely reviewed of any personal Holocaust story in the United States. His voice speaks with coherence, and has come into prominence along with his international recognition as a "successful" Holocaust survivor and witness. Recipient of the Nobel Peace Prize and of over eighty-five honorary doctoral degrees, he embodies the hero of the quest narrative, one who has endured hell and returned to speak with knowledge and wisdom for peace. He is truly the author of his work, writing, rewriting and editing his story, and rebutting challenges to the veracity of his words.

The response to *Night* cannot be separated from Wiesel as a person who allows us to believe in a successful outcome of not only survival, but of fame and goodness: The traditional autobiography has hardly ever been a medium for victims. On the contrary, it's been a repository for winners, those born that way or those who made it against the odds (Johnston, in Miller 1994, pp. 18, 19).

His public life parallels autobiographical conventions as the story of a cultural hero, a public figure who "triumphs over myriad impediments" (Gergen and Gergen, 1993, pp. 195, 196). The fates of Wiesel's words have followed many of the conventions of Western writing, including those of the quest narrative:

> mythic heroism . . . evidenced not by force of arms but by *perseverance* . . . the truth that has been learned is prophetic, often carrying demands for social action . . . These writers . . . want to use suffering to move others forward with them. . . . [Their stories turn lived experience] into a paradigm of universal conflicts and concerns. (Frank 1995, pp. 119, 121, 126)

Wiesel fits Gergen and Gergen's convention of Western auto/biographical convention, that holds that one successful life story can embody an entire historical event or period:

> [P]opular . . . . autobiographical figures represent a culturally and historically situate [sic] model of an ideal self. . . . the saga of a hero who triumphs over myriad impediments. . . . this account

> of the autobiography is most relevant to—if not the unique prov-
> enance of—prominent public figures; in almost all cases, the high
> status man. (1993, p. 195)

There is no comparably well-known female voice of survival.

Anne Frank's story fits other conventions of life writing. Her story speaks for the millions murdered and her memory is evoked worldwide whenever people want to emphasize the senselessness of the Holocaust and bravery in the face of death. Her life and death have entered the life stories of many Holocaust writers. Fania Fenelon, a survivor of Auschwitz, writes of her time at Bergen-Belsen shortly before liberation:

> Soldiers began to improvise a sort of gigantic tent, almost at
> ground level . . . We lay down, drenched to the skin, shivering, but
> we were in such a state of exhaustion that we fell asleep. . . . I was
> later to learn that, a few yards from me, Anne Frank was lying
> under this same canvas. (p. 239)

I can easily read Anne Frank's diary as a quest narrative: she suffers and dies, but leaves words that inspire others. Because these written words end before Auschwitz, when I read her story I have to remind myself that, after her entry of August 1, 1944, Anne Frank was arrested and sent to Westerbork, Auschwitz, and Bergen-Belsen, where she died of typhus. In particular, the theatrical production of her diary, with its triumphant ending and affirmation of the goodness of humanity, tempts me to hold her written life as an exemplar of how to live and show courage in the face of death. I can bracket the horrors of Westerbork, Auschwitz, and Bergen-Belsen and imagine Anne Frank going to her death with her spirit undefeated.

In telling the story of a young woman who never reached adulthood, Frank's diary points beyond itself to countless losses wreaked by the Holocaust on all of humanity—words she never wrote, talents she never expressed as an adult woman, and other lives terminated before giving voice to their unique gifts and talents. I feel this loss deeply and personally, and can only respond with sorrow by honoring the words we do have.[4]

The popularity of Frank's diary also lies in the fact that it is a semi-private diary. Even though the most personal entries were removed from early translations, this young girl's diary—chatty, introspective, and personal, articulate and discerning—corresponded to my adolescent ideals for the most celebrated female story of the Holocaust.[5]

REPRESENTATIVE STORIES?

An individual story, whether of a murdered victim or of one survivor, is infinitely more accessible to the imagination and emotions than a report of mass suffering. Perhaps a couple of voices are most appropriate for telling of Auschwitz or the Holocaust. As Auschwitz survivor Ka-Tzetnik 135633 wrote in the postscript to *Moni: A Novel of Auschwitz* or *Atrocity*:

> Rudolph Hoes, the Commandant, has stated that 2,000,000 men, women and children were burned in Auschwitz. The tragedy of these zeros is impossible to comprehend . . . I have told part of the story of the two million in the life and death of one small boy. (1987)

Moreover, Auschwitz stories tell of dehumanization that all but obliterated individual differences. Elie Wiesel asserted a remarkable uniformity in Auschwitz stories: "They seem to have been written by one man, always the same, repeating a thousand times what you, the reader, even if you are his contemporary, will never understand" (1978, p. 200). The notion of a representative story of victim or survivor resonates in and through Elie Wiesel's words, and in the canonical nature that has come to characterize *Night* and *The Diary of Anne Frank*. Each tells of the Holocaust through one voice, a particular story that "is perhaps close enough to shared experience to justify the telling" (Schweickart 1991, p. 525).

Perhaps this is fitting. Perhaps differences in telling amount to mere nuances, and to emphasize them would tell a false tale of individual choice in situations of what Langer has called "choiceless choices" (1991). Perhaps Auschwitz engulfed individual differences, whether of gender, nationality, or intellect.

Perhaps.

There are, however, inherent weaknesses in privileging a particular story or in assuming that there is a single story to be told. From the perspective of a single representative voice, divergent Holocaust voices are "Other" and therefore marginal to many conversations about the Holocaust. If I generalize from Frank's and Wiesel's stories, I minimize the essential humanity of all Holocaust victims. As Joan Ringelheim reminds me, there is no one story of Auschwitz. "[N]o two Jews experienced what is called the Holocaust in quite the same way . . . There is no time, there is no place that is the same for everyone, not even Auschwitz" (1990, p. 143). By the fact of their existence, women's life stories counter representative male "auto/biography,"[6] for "women's textual and published lives are made against the grain of exemplary *male* lives, whose implied universalism is thereby rejected" (Stanley 1993, p. 46).[7] Collectively, emphasis on the distinctiveness of survivor voices, particularly women's voices, challenges the notion that only celebrated lives are worthy of record.

A CHALLENGE

When Elie Wiesel and Anne Frank first penned their stories, they wrote not from the center of a dominant culture, but from the margins and in opposition to the tyrannical voice of Nazi fascism. But their words are anything but marginal today.[8] By every measure that I undertook, *Night* and *Anne Frank: The Diary of a Young Girl* have been canonized by scholars and the media. Their rise to prominence places them far from the perimeters of Holocaust discourse.[9]

I needed to listen more closely to the voices of victims and survivors speaking from the margins of Holocaust conversations. Since each life story is thus not *the* story of a life, but *many* stories, I could not come close to understanding it unless I broadened my reading horizons. I also wanted to know more about the unique aspects of women's Auschwitz stories, and what their words add to my understanding of the Holocaust. Charlotte Delbo, Fania Fenelon and Sara Nomberg-Przytyk spoke to me most powerfully, articulately, and authentically.

NOTES

1. See Alvin Rosenfeld's "Popularization and Memory: The Case of Anne Frank" for a discussion of the increasing scope and intensity with which the 1989 fiftieth anniversary of her birth has sparked an outpouring of media attention on "the most famous child of the twentieth century" (1991, p. 244). Rosenfeld also argues that Frank's story has also powerfully entered collective memory through the play, "The Diary of Anne Frank."

2. All quotes of Frank are from this edition unless otherwise indicated.

3. The 1995 Doubleday edition of Frank's diary, as well as the original diary itself, include the phrase "as Jews" here, but earlier editions omit the phrase.

4. Thank you to Carolyn Ellis and Arthur Bochner for bringing this point to my attention.

5. There exist male diaries of the Holocaust—in particular several from the Warsaw Ghetto—but these take on the form of public records, intended and constituted as historical documents or as documentation of personal thoughts of an already famous man such as the radio personality and pediatrician Janusz Korczak (Cameron, et al., 1993). Anne's diary is more personal, more private.

6. The term "auto/biography," as used by the British Sociological Association Auto/Biography Study Group and its journal, captures the complex intertextuality between various forms and genres of life stories.

7. Stanley draws from Robert Merton's (1977) work on "prosopography" or the sociological study of life stories, and suggests that auto/biography is a source of insiders' knowledge, valid and distinct from outsiders' knowledge. Auto/biography is "text . . . a topic for investigation in its own right, and not as a resource to tell us about something lying outside the text itself" (p. 43).

8. All stories are dynamic, informed by the socio-historic contexts within which they are produced and read. Thus, it is not surprising to find scholarship on Holocaust texts evolving. Various developments in interpretation offer their own insights; and each text is a different text in different times and places.

9. Lyotard writes of the Holocaust that "no individual or group has authority in this manner" (1990, p. xiv). However, my readings of Holocaust memoirs and scholarship demonstrate that some do assume or are granted great authority in this manner.

CHAPTER 3
Different Horrors

Journal Entry: February 13, 1992

I am reading a story told by Charlotte Delbo—partisan, Frenchwoman, Auschwitz survivor, and playwright. Her words are shaped into a poignant poetic drama titled *None of Us Will Return*. They have an immediacy far stronger than any chronological telling could have. As she weaves past and present together, she envelops me in a tapestry from which I cannot escape. Lately, I have been having nightmares about Auschwitz. In these dreams, I am always in the camp with my children. I panic as I try to save their lives. I put aside her words and my writing for a few days to regain some distance. Doing so only reminds me that this is a luxury not accessible to Delbo. Her dreams are memories from which she will never escape.

I identify more closely with Delbo than I have with other survivors whose words I have read or heard. True, most of the Holocaust stories I have read so far have been written by men. But there is more than her woman's voice drawing me to her. Like me, she was not Jewish. Like me, she had a deep respect and love for words. While my Calvinist tradition valued The Word as the repository of truth, Delbo's approach respects words as references to truths. She does not flinch from nor explain away death and *chaos. Delbo tells just enough of her own story to illuminate the humanity of the prisoners who became her life-giving friends. I have much to learn from her.*

Tricia Meade, then a student in the Honors College at Western Michigan University, first introduced me to Charlotte Delbo in 1992. She lent me a musty 1968 library copy of *None of Us Will Return.* I coveted a copy of my own, but it was out of print. I searched for more women's Auschwitz stories and speculated as to why stories such as Delbo's were so hard to find.

I began my study of Auschwitz stories at a time in my life when I was enamored with what now seems a simple but crucial understanding of feminist reading and scholarship. After spending over fifteen years in nursing, earning bachelor's and master's degrees in the field, working for over eight years in community health, and experiencing a growing restlessness and drive to understand societal contexts for my life, I began a doctoral program in sociology. I felt as if I'd come home. I found the option for qualitative methodology much more compelling, relevant, and truer to my experiences than the quantitative work I'd done to earn my master's degree. I was quickly drawn to interdisciplinary cultural studies, Robert Merton's approach to sociology as the intersection of biography and history, and the excitement of listening closely to women's voices as theorists, writers of fiction, and authors of their life stories. Cultural studies gave me language tools to name what I was reading.

In this chapter I tell of this search and my first careful reading of six survivors' stories. This reading is neatly analytic, supported by a satisfaction that the stories confirmed a particular feminist template that I'd brought with me. This reading, which I later found to be incomplete, nonetheless lays a necessary foundation for the subsequent and more complex readings that follow in Chapters Four and Five.

Although approximately half of all first-person Auschwitz stories available in English are written by women, most of these have received scant academic or public attention. A few examples illustrate a consistent pattern of marginalization of women's voices—

with the exception of Anne Frank's. A computerized English-language FirstSearch of books and articles on March 9, 1998, including data bases from WorldCat, The Modern Language Association, Article List, Periodic Abstracts, Biographical Index, and Dissertation Abstracts shows thirty-two for Delbo, eighteen for Nomberg-Przytyk, and only seven for Fenelon. In contrast, these same sources have 1193 *WorldCat* entries for Anne Frank, 566 for Elie Wiesel, and 256 for Levi. Two of the male survivors I've been reading are only lightly covered by these sources–there are thirty-one entries for Jean Amery and twenty-two for Szymon Laks–but are reviewed more extensively in French, German, and Polish publications.

A collection of Holocaust and genocide syllabi, published by the American Sociological Association (Porter 1992), shows two listings for Delbo and one for Nomberg-Przytyk. Goldenberg's syllabus in the ASA document lists all three in her extensive bibliography of literature of the Holocaust. Yet the words of these survivors are relegated to footnotes, a chapter in a book, a single session at a conference, or a cloistered collection of their words (Lagerwey 1993, 1994; Markle et al., 1992).

Well-known Holocaust scholars Lawrence Langer (1975) and James Young (1988) do mention works by women–including Charlotte Delbo, Fania Fenelon and Sara Nomberg-Przytyk–in their analyses of Holocaust personal narratives.[1] Neither, however, examines female or male Holocaust stories as gendered voices. Langer's (1991) work on memory, for example, categorizes Holocaust testimony as a unified body of literature. While he promotes women's writings such as Delbo's Auschwitz trilogy, he is less helpful in identifying what is unique to women's experiences in the Holocaust.

My reaction to the relative paucity of attention paid to women's Holocaust writings followed a path worn by others. Marlene Heinemann summarized this critique:

> The study of Holocaust literature has focused primarily on the writings of men, whose perspectives have been taken as representative of the experience of all Holocaust victims. But to assume that Holocaust literature by men represents the writings of women is

to remain blind to the findings of scholarship about the significance
of gender in history and literature. (1986, p. 2)

I concur with Myrna Goldenberg who argued that we need
to listen more carefully to women's voices from the Holocaust.
In her paper, "Different Horrors, Same Hell: Women Remembering the Holocaust," she articulates the framework used in
this chapter:

> English language audiences know Holocaust literature prima-
> rily through male writers and have generalized those experiences
> to represent the whole. . . . Narratives by women survivors, how-
> ever, form a group that differs significantly from those by men. .
> . . We are obliged to examine, separately, the lives of women and
> of men to determine the differences in the way they were treated
> as well as in the way they responded. (1990, pp. 150, 152)

In most Holocaust scholarship, "the particularities of women's
experiences and reflections [on the Holocaust] have been sub-
merged and ignored" (Rittner and Roth 1993, p. xi).

While women's Holocaust stories are publicly available, it is
only since the early 1980s that their distinctiveness has been paid
serious and systematic attention. Des Pres briefly contrasts female
survivors' experiences with men's, and concludes in a letter that
"under infinitely more terrible circumstances, women in places
like Auschwitz and Ravensbruck made better survivors" (in
Ringelheim 1984, p. 72).

As the larger overall realities of the Holocaust have entered
the "stock of common knowledge" (using Berger and Luckmann's
terms, 1966), a second generation of Holocaust scholarship has
paid increasing attention to a wide range of differences in existing
and emerging stories–differences between concentration camps,
between religious and secular Jews, between Jews and non-Jews,
between nationalities, and between women and men. This develop-
ment began with a recognition that women's Holocaust writings
had been largely ignored, and that these writings told significantly
different stories than those told by men. Marked by the first
conference on "Women Surviving the Holocaust" in March 1983
(Katz and Ringelheim 1983), questions of gender have become
more central to Holocaust conversations.[2]

Literature about women's lives and their stories gave me an organizing language or template for reading. Scenes from women's Auschwitz stories illustrated similar patterns: permeable ego-boundaries, affective nurturing, interpersonal relationships, and the domestic private sphere, or in the words of The Personal Narrative Group, an interdisciplinary group of feminist scholars at Indiana University, "the special reliance of women upon the resources of networks of family and kin, and the important role women play in nurturing and maintaining such networks" (1989, p. 21):

> [I]n contrast to men's accounts, women's story lines are multiple, intermingled, ambivalent as to valence, and recursive. Whereas men's stories concentrate on the pursuit of single goals, most often career oriented, women's are more complex. . . . Women's forms are deviant. (Gergen and Gergen, 1993, p. 195–96)

This template highlights contrasting patterns in men's stories as well: unemotional intellect, instrumental rationality, public spheres of action, separateness, differentiation, autonomy and independence (Chodorow 1978; Durkheim 1912; Heilbrun 1989; Mason 1980; Miller 1991, 1994; Sydie 1987). My path in reading Auschwitz stories with an eye to expected contrasts between women's and men's words does not feel like a solitary one. Many others have gone before me in demonstrating that the experiences of women and men at Auschwitz (and their accounts of their experiences) were not only separate, but qualitatively distinct. Not only do female narratives differ in style from male narratives, but until the final chaotic months before liberation, these women and men worked, ate, slept, and died apart from each other, and thus write about different experiences. From selection ramps on arrival to death, women and men were separated in the camps. Owing to the setting and to "their biology, i.e., as childbearers, and their socialization, i.e., as nurturers and homemakers" (Goldenberg 1990, p. 151) their stories differ.

The works of Marlene Heinemann (1986), Ellen Fine (1990), Mary and Kenneth Gergen (1993), Myrna Goldenberg (1990), Ruth Linden (1993), Sybil Milton (1984), Joan Ringelheim (1984, 1985, 1990, 1993) and Nechama Tec (1993), for example, speak

powerfully to the importance of gender in the event and scholarship of the Holocaust. Many have concluded that women's modes
of survival were superior. Sybil Milton (1984) describes gendered
patterns among the everyday lives of prisoners in Nazi concentration camps: hunger, food, housekeeping, and mutually supportive
networks.[3] Marlene Heinemann (1986) analyzes women's Holocaust narratives from a variety of genres and identifies themes of
sexuality, intimacy, and authenticity. There were three particular
sex-based problems for women: sexual abuse and humiliation,
including rape and prostitution; menstruation and amenorrhea,
with related fears of humiliation and infertility; and maternity and
childbirth. Her analysis also considers genre, authenticity, subjectivity, literary norms, and canon. Ellen Fine (1990) draws attention
to themes of maternity and childbirth, mothers and children in
Holocaust stories, and notes the effects these had on chances of
survival. She argues that women's use of literature in communal
settings in concentration camps "was a life-sustaining force, a means
of bonding and support, of moral and spiritual sustenance" (p. 93).

More recently, Raul Hilberg (1992) and Irena Strzelecka (1994)
also mentioned the pivotal but complex role gender played
throughout the Holocaust. Works such as Carol Rittner and John
Roth's (1993) collection of women's Holocaust stories addressed
the question "Where are the women?" and began to correct the
deficiency by providing an avenue through which women's voices
could be heard.

Gergen and Gergen point to the necessity of reading all texts
through gendered lenses. They emphasize the close identification
of women with their bodies, and the consequent fact that "vio-
lations of the body are defacements of identity, and so are invest-
ments of the body in others' modes of unifying self and other"
(1994, p. 212). They contrast women's embodiment with a male
pattern of minimizing the "significance of intimates" noting as we
find in Wiesel's writings that "the major exception to this general
disregard is the father's death, which often receives considerable
attention. The importance of the father's death can be traced to
the threat it symbolizes to the male portrayal of invulnerability"
(1993, p. 213).

It was a conclusion I made embarrassingly slowly, that all Auschwitz stories are gendered–as indeed is all writing (Mason, in Miller 1994; Swindells 1989), and must be read through lenses of gender. As with all stories, those from Auschwitz–whether told by women or by men, recognized or not–are shaped by gender.[4]

Journal Entry: February 2, 1994

I have driven two and a half hours to Chicago, to the Speritus Museum to see Judy Chicago's "Holocaust Project" Exhibition. I purchased her book, *The Holocaust Project: From Darkness into Light* (1993) about the exhibit several weeks ago, and have been eager to see the actual displays. The project is a multimedia story of her encounters with Holocaust stories and of her rediscovery of her Jewish identity.

It's midweek, late morning and there are only half a dozen other visitors there. I start by visiting other exhibits, in particular the children's art work on the war in Bosnia, and work my way around to the main exhibit.

I begin with a half-hour video made by Judy and her husband, photographer Donald Woodman, with whom she has collaborated on the project. The headphones that accompany the tour are again in Chicago's voice, and an integral part of the project. I take about two hours to tour the exhibit. It is a broadly collaborative work, utilizing the skills of many "artisans" in layers of texture and time.

Chicago's work, especially a piece titled "Double Jeopardy" powerfully speaks to me of ways in which Jewish women were doubly oppressed—by both ethnicity and sex—a point Chicago argues is often overlooked in other verbal and visual representations of the Holocaust. I am less comfortable with the celebratory message of her final piece, a multicultural "Rainbow Chabbat." The work is beautifully done in stained glass, a life-size depiction of joyful celebration. Perhaps it suggests a happy ending

*in which I do not believe. I am also disappointed by her undeviating
portrayals of women in conventional guises: seamstresses, mothers,
matriarchs, victims of rape.*

*I do not agree with Chicago's critics who argue that the story of
the "Holocaust Project" is too removed from Chicago's family and
experience to claim as her own. I know that the immediacy of
Holocaust stories extends far beyond those who directly
encountered the event. I think too of how the Holocaust has
become part of the intellectual stories of many of us, and of the
variety of texts and media we use to tell these stories.*

STORY AND GENDER

While suffering and death did not respect individual attributes
within Auschwitz, they did act within gendered coordinates. Nazi
ideology, propaganda, and literature drew the parameters of life
and death, of choice and non-choice, over a template of biologi-
cally based classifications—lineage, gender and individual devia-
tions from the Aryan norm. Its ideology drew from and encouraged a complex mix of anti-Semitism and sexism. Furthermore,
for those who survived initial selection upon arrival at Auschwitz,
gender set parameters for realities of life and death which followed,
and for the stories of those who witnessed these events. Witnesses'
stories are not disembodied chronologies. They are also stories
told by gendered beings to a gendered world.

Early on in my readings of Auschwitz stories, especially in
discussions with two friends, Joanne and Katie, I found myself
speaking repeatedly of the differences I found in women's stories.
Each of us has studied women's life-stories, each from a different
discipline. One summer day, over lunch, I took my pen and
outlined on a paper napkin a series of pairs of survivors, female
and male, and the patterns of differences I found in comparing
and contrasting stories within and between these pairs. This ar-
tifact remains tucked away with piles of research notes, a reminder
of an early turning point on my journey.

I told these friends about the moment when I first read Fenelon's story of singing for the SS as a story of rape, and understood it in contrast to Laks' description of camaraderie of bridge games and music with the Germans. We agreed: giving music is rightly akin to physical love; but in extremity—in Fenelon's story—it has been twisted into the moral equivalent of rape. The contrasting stories of playing music powerfully demonstrate the particular fears, risks, and indignities to which the women were subjected at Auschwitz. This method worked well for drawing attention to differences between women's and men's writings. I could pair the stories of six survivors, based on their position within Auschwitz or on their style of writing, and use the stories to contrast women's and men's Auschwitz stories.

It was a small step from my personal thoughts to concurring that women's voices had been largely ignored in Holocaust studies, that their experiences were substantially different from men's, and that they exhibited superior survival skills. In the reading that follows, I re-tell the stories that most closely correspond to the patterns of this two-dimensional template. I easily found evidence in Auschwitz stories of women's unique experiences, of sexuality, friendship and parenting, their mutual concern for and assistance of each other, their emotional capacity, their unselfish and sacrificial sharing, and great flexibility—in sum, a moral superiority that even the horrors of Auschwitz could not obliterate. And, true to my expectations, I found that the stories written by men told of personal isolation, personal survival at any cost, ruthless competition, and pragmatic allegiances. Male survivors framed their narratives in order and coherence, and often de-emphasized emotions.

The following reading of gendered pairs of survivors' stories furnishes ample examples of ways in which these stories reflect the gendered realities of life and death in Auschwitz, and the gendered identities of the witnesses. Perhaps it is no surprise that these patterns reflect many general patterns found in women's personal narratives, regardless of context.

Sara Nomberg-Przytyk and Primo Levi

Sara Nomberg-Przytyk and Primo Levi were professional writers after the war. Nomberg-Przytyk was a journalist by trade, while Levi, who was a chemist, "retired" from his position at the Turin paint factory in 1974 in order to write full-time. Nomberg-Przytyk and Levi are at their literary best when they speak through the voices and stories of others. They approach truths indirectly, taking the reader on a narrated and open-ended tour of a photo album labeled "Auschwitz." A professional writer at the time of his death, Levi credits Auschwitz with his decision to write. He describes the initial need to write about the Holocaust in his "Author's Preface" to *Survival in Auschwitz*:

> As an account of atrocities, therefore, this book of mine adds nothing to what is already known to readers throughout the world on the disturbing questions of the death camps. It has not been written in order to formulate new accusations; it should be able, rather, to furnish documentation for a quiet study of certain aspects of the human mind. . . .
>
> The need to tell our story to "the rest," to make "the rest" participate in it, had taken on for us, before our liberation and after, the character of an immediate and violent impulse, to the point of competing with our other elementary needs. The book has been written to satisfy this need: first and foremost, therefore, as an interior liberation. (1961, p. 5)

Nomberg-Przytyk's style of reportage finds its way into her tale of Auschwitz. The stories themselves, often told through the voices of other inmates, demand telling. They are immediate, bound by time and place. She asks that the reader "[l]isten to the story I am going to tell you and then you can tell what you think" (p. 110). She continues to write as a reporter, telling the stories of other prisoners: "this is what we heard" (p. 108); "This was the story of the young French girl. We listened to the story as if we were hearing the most beautiful music" (p. 109); "Mrs. Helena finished her terrible tale" (p. 113); "I kept overhearing scraps of his story" (p. 160). She writes, editors Eli Pfefferkorn and David Hirsch tell me in their Editor's Afterword, "in the tradition of the Yiddish folktale" (1998, p. 169).

Nomberg-Przytyk juxtaposes stories of individual women with a chorus of women who live, breath, and die as one. As they are forced to stand and watch the execution of Mala, a "heroine" who had attempted to escape, "one enormous sigh was heaved from their collective breasts . . . 'Mala, Mala'—a whisper issued from a thousand lips like a single sigh" (p. 103). They listen helplessly to children screaming "Mama!" as they are being burned to death, and "a scream of despair tore out of our throats, growing louder all the time" (p. 82).

Levi's stories have a quality of timelessness. His tales are universal in scope, a re-telling of the grand narratives of creation, good, and evil. In his last work, Levi also speaks reflexively of his lifelong adventure of story-telling:

> I will tell just one more story, the most secret, and I will tell it with the humility and restraint of him who knows from the start that this theme is desperate, the means feeble, and the trade of clothing facts in words is bound by its very nature to fail. (1988, p. xx)

Levi's style of writing and the themes that permeate his stories incorporate what I thought of as a traditional male narrative pattern, emphasizing authority, universal themes, and coherence of form. He tells the reader that he wrote his first account of Auschwitz "not in logical succession, but in order of urgency" (1961, p. 6), later arranging the manuscript in chronological order.

Levi speaks with great borrowed authority when he uses the metaphor of the captivity in Egypt. He prefaces his first book with a paraphrase of Moses' words to the Israelites shortly after the Exodus, as recorded in Deuteronomy. He writes:

> Meditate that this came about/ I commend these words to you/ Carve them in your hearts/ At home, in the street/ Going to bed, rising/ Repeat them to your children/ Or may your house fall apart/ May illness impede you/ May your children turn their faces from you. (1961, p. 8)

In the women's stories I found fewer authoritative pronouncements and more scenes of human affection.

For Nomberg-Przytyk, human connections and stories are the essence of what it means to be human. To be human is to love and be loved, to have a story. She weaves together themes of human meaning, situated physicality, and reflection on the act of writing. The women of Auschwitz take on the flesh of humanity when Nomberg-Przytyk conceives of a past, a story for each. "I tried to imagine," she writes of the faceless women of the *Leichenkomando* "whose job it was to load the dead into the trucks . . . what kind of women they had been a few years ago, when they loved and were loved" (p. 115). She humanizes the dead in her tales, imagining their full lives before Auschwitz:

> . . . what bothered me most in my desperate situation were the naked decaying corpses lying in front of the block. Every morning the *sztubowe* pulled the dead women out of the beds. She immediately stripped them naked, dragged them through the whole block, and heaved them into the mud. As she dragged them through the whole block by one hand you could hear the bones crack, and the loosely hanging heads banged on the cement. I thought in despair that these might have been highly intelligent, talented beings— actresses, painters, poets. Or maybe they were just women who loved and were loved in return. Maybe they had children to whom they were most beautiful. Maybe they were dreamers. (p. 22)

It is painful for Nomberg-Przytyk to recognize the common humanity she shares with these women. They are not unlike her. She writes, "I was frightened by the thought that tomorrow they would be dragging me through the block, a nameless dishonored corpse, unmourned by anyone" (p. 22).

Nomberg-Przytyk shudders in silent rebellion at the sexist logic that believed that youth and beauty could buy a reprieve from death by gas. She watches a young woman being selected for death and wonders, "'she is really young and pretty. Why did they write her number down?' I trembled at that terrible logic, as though there were some justification in killing the sick, the elderly, and the unattractive" (p. 29). Systems by which we unthinkingly assign worth to others are to her not merely unkind, they are sinister and deadly.

In Levi's stories, however, women are matter-of-factly seen from a distance, nameless and typecast. There are few female characters in Levi's tales, in fact, "[i]n those days it rarely happened that one saw a woman close up, an experience both tender and savage that left you shattered" (1979, p. 40). When Levi speaks of women, they seem only abstractly embodied. They remain separate, within a private realm of maternal nurturing—a world on a collision course with the public world of death. Mothers care for their children in preparation for a one-way trip to Auschwitz. "[T]he mothers stayed up to prepare the food for the journey with tender care. . . . Would you not do the same? If you and your child were going to be killed tomorrow, would you not give him to eat today?" (1959, p. 11).

In the midst of his Auschwitz tale, Levi curiously presents the mythic story of Lilith, perhaps the first wife of Adam, perhaps the scandalous lover of God. This story, on first reading incongruous with the realities of Auschwitz, situates Auschwitz within a legendary tale. On their shared birthday, the "Tischler" (carpenter) tells Levi stories of Lilith to explore mysteries of creation, sex and evil—and of Auschwitz. In one story God has taken Lilith as a mistress because his wife, the Shekhina, has left him in anger over the destruction of the Temple in Jerusalem. He concludes:

> . . . you must know that this obscene tryst has not ended, and won't end soon. In one way it's the cause of the evil that occurs on earth; in another way, it is its effect. As long as God continues to sin with Lilith, there will be blood and trouble on Earth. But one day a powerful being will come—the one we are all waiting for. He will make Lilith die and put an end to God's lechery, and to our exile. (1986, p. 44)

Unlike the male characters in Levi's stories, Lilith is the object, not the subject, of the story. To the male gaze Lilith is the mysterious embodiment of the complexities of life itself. Levi chooses not to grant the gift of subjectivity to Lilith. It is not her story. Lilith, an icon of womanhood, is "Other"—not fully human.[5]

Many scenes in Nomberg-Przytyk's and Levi's stories fulfilled my initial expectations for gendered differences. Nomberg-Przytyk writes with less detachment, and with more emphasis on interpersonal networks of caring. She also powerfully addresses women's unique sexual concerns, particularly pregnancy and childbirth. Although, as I argue later, Levi does write about close interpersonal friendships among individual men, he tells his own and others' stories dispassionately, with a clear and rational cynicism. In his telling, the men at Auschwitz found little cause for redemption, reassuring insights into the human condition, or personal growth through suffering.

Charlotte Delbo and Jean Amery

Born just one year apart, in 1913 and 1912 respectively, Charlotte Delbo and Jean Amery were two agnostic intellectuals, arrested in 1942 for their roles in resistance movements, sent to prison and subsequently to Auschwitz. Their Auschwitz manuscripts appeared in print just one year apart, Delbo's in 1965 and Amery's in 1966. Both published extensively in Europe after liberation, and are recently gaining audiences in the United States.

In contrast to other survivors, neither Delbo nor Amery writes specifically about their positions in Auschwitz. Amery does not write about his position at all, except to emphasize that it was not one of privilege. He speaks of himself as an "unskilled laborer" (p. 3) and one of "the anonymous mass of the prisoners" (p. 6). Delbo, a non-Jew, writes of being assigned easier work than the Jewish women. She offers hints, writing first person vignettes of collective work. She tells us that for some time at Auschwitz "we worked in a laboratory a few kilometers from the big camp. . . . We were glad to be there because it meant we could wash, have clean clothes, work in a sheltered situation" (p. 158). And later, "In the shop the sewing machines were stitching jackets and more jackets, by the hundreds. . . . The only way to slow down the chain was to break one's needle. . . Each one of us would break her needle in turn" (p. 189).

Delbo, a non-Jewish member of the French resistance, was imprisoned in Auschwitz in January 1943. She wrote her story immediately after her liberation, waited twenty years to have it published, and told one of her English translators, "I wanted to make sure it would withstand the test of time, since it had to travel far into the future" (quoted in Lamont 1990, p. x).

Much of Delbo's writing contradicts the notion that Auschwitz was characterized by ruthless individualism. She describes the women she came to know at Auschwitz: "There were eight of us, perched on a narrow platform, a group of eight friends death would separate" (p. 17). Delbo reflects:

> It was important not to be separated from one's group. We had to leave together or remain together. Each one of us had experienced fully the fact than an isolated individual is defenseless, that

you cannot survive without the others. By "the others" we meant those members of our group who hold you up, or carry you when you can no longer walk, those who help you hold fast when you're at the end of your rope. (p. 193)

At times Delbo uses a metaphor of a human body to talk about all women prisoners, regardless of their diverse backgrounds: "We stood there motionless, several thousand women speaking a variety of languages from all over, huddled together. . . . reduced to our heartbeats" (p. 25). Death, too, is universal. "The women lying there in the snow are yesterday's companions" (p. 18). Delbo's net of inclusiveness is broad. She begins the second part of her trilogy with a chapter entitled "The Men" by telling of the deep relatedness and tenderness the women felt for the men, and of the women's deliberate pose of patience and courage:

[The women's] femininity safeguarded them, as was still believed. And if they, the men, had everything to fear, the women found reassurance in being women. All they needed was patience and courage, two virtues they were certain to possess since these were part of everyday life. So they comforted the men by not allowing exhaustion, distress, and above all anxiety to surface. . . . Although their distress was just as great, the women still had some resources, those always possessed by women. They could do the wash, mend the shirt, now in tatters, the men wore the day of their arrest, cut up blankets to make booties. They deprived themselves a portion of bread to give it to the men. A man must eat more. Every Sunday, they staged an entertainment in the prison yard, which the men could watch standing behind the barbed-wire fence erected between the two quarters. All week the women were hard at work sewing and rehearsing for the coming Sunday. When the entertainment's preparation was threatened by the sinking of the spirit, or a bad mood, a woman was always there to say: "We've got to do it for the men." For the men, they sang and danced, putting on a merry, carefree air. (p. 118)

For Delbo, the vast category of comrade expands to include women, men, and the earth itself. She tells us: "In the spring men and women sprinkle ashes on drained marshland plowed for the first time. They fertilize the soil with human phosphates. . . . people are needed to drain the marshes and cover them with the others' ashes" (p. 9). She gives us here a grotesque image of nature cyclicly renewing itself as it cannibalistically feeds off the ashes of comrades to which all are reduced.

At other times Delbo uses less ominous images to represent humanity's solidarity. Her long poetic lists of new arrivals, reminiscent of Whitman's catalogues of workers in "Leaves of Grass," include women and men from every corner of the continent:

> Some came from Warsaw wearing large shawls and with tied-up bundles/ some from Zagreb, the women their heads covered by scarves/ some from the Danube wearing multicolored woolen sweaters through long night hours/ some from Greece, they took with them black olives and loukoums/ . . . all of them regret that they could not have stopped home to change into something less dainty. (pp. 5–6)

Amery, too, catalogues the inmates of Auschwitz—but by their professions: craftsmen, businessmen, professors, lawyers, librarians, economists, and mathematicians (pp. 3–4). Women are noticeably absent from his list. In fact, he never mentions the women of Auschwitz. Never one with the other prisoners—male or female—Amery writes of his moral and social isolation:

> The rejection of the SS logic, the revolt that turned inward, the muted murmuring of such incantations as: "But that is not possible" did not last long. After a certain time there inevitably appeared something that was more than mere resignation and that we may designate as an acceptance not only of the SS logic but also of the SS system of values. And once again the intellectual prisoner had it harder than the unintellectual. For the latter there had never been a universal humane logic, rather only a consistent system of self-preservation. . . . For him the camp logic was merely the step-by-step intensification of economic logic, and one opposed this intensification with a useful mixture of resignation and the readiness to defend oneself. (p. 10)

Amery writes of the logic of self-preservation and the dissonance created for him as an intellectual. He clearly states that he writes as an individual, but only within contexts of larger abstract issues. The first person "I" of his intensely personal reflections easily shifts to the third person "the victim." In the "Preface to the First Edition" of *Beyond the Mind's Limits* he describes the processes of his writing about Auschwitz: "Confessing and medi-

tating, I arrived at an examination or, if you will, a phenomenological description of the existence of the victim" (p. xxiv). As with
the hero of a quest narrative, he returns to a post-Auschwitz world
forever changed, with truths that demand to be told:

> We did not become wiser in Auschwitz, if by wisdom one
> understands positive knowledge of the world. . . . We did not become
> "deeper," if that calamitous depth is at all a definable intellectual
> quantity. It goes without saying, I believe, that in Auschwitz we did
> not become better, more human, more humane, and more mature
> ethically. . . . We lost a good deal of arrogance, of metaphysical
> conceit, but also quite a bit of our naive joy in the intellect and
> what we falsely imagined was the sense of life. . . . And so I dare
> to say that we didn't leave Auschwitz wiser and deeper, but we
> were no doubt smarter. (pp. 19–20)

What he has learned will not redeem society, but it is an absolute
truth reaching far beyond the lived experiences of a single individual. His inability to speak the camp slang, the only accepted
form of communication between prisoners, exacerbates his loneliness:

> In a conversation with a bunkmate, for instance, who talked
> at length about his wife's daily menu, he [the intellectual] was
> anxious to slip in the observation that at home he himself had done
> lots of reading. But when for the thirtieth time he received the
> answer: "Shit, man!"–he left off. (pp. 6–7)

Amery writes of universal realities but remains engulfed in loneliness.

While talk of literature and an intellectual stance only isolate
Amery from other prisoners, literature is indispensable to Delbo
and her friends, and a means of resisting isolation. The women
recite plays while they work, repeating the lines until all have
memorized them. In January 1943, they put on a play drawn
from memory, Moliere's *Le Malade Imaginaire* (*The Imaginary In-
valid*). Charlotte Delbo directs. They know how incongruous this
is, for "we were living our last illusion" (p. 169). They perform
for other women prisoners, and Delbo concludes, "It was
magnificent. . . . It was magnificent because, for the space of two
hours, while the smokestacks never stopped belching their smoke
of human flesh, for two whole hours we believed in what we were

doing" (p. 171). The play and the world outside which it represents are treasures to be shared. Thus, on another day, Delbo trades a ration of bread, the universal currency of Auschwitz, for a small book, Moliere's *Misanthrope*. She returns breadless to her barracks comrades who are spreading their bread with margarine for supper. Delbo tells them of her purchase, and "Each one of my companions cut a slice of bread from her ration" (p. 188). The women beg Delbo to read to them. The treasure is communal yet highly personal. Delbo memorized the play and tells us, "until departure, I kept the play within my throat" (p. 188).

Delbo temporarily bridges the chasm between the nightmare of Auschwitz and the world before with poetry and images familiar to women: motherhood, pregnancy and children, flowers, mannequins from clothing stores. She isolates simple camp experiences and universalizes the affective component of the detail. She writes:

> O you who know/did you know that you can see your mother dead/ and not shed a tear/. . . O you who know/ did you know that a day is longer than a year/ a minute longer than a lifetime/ . . . O you who know/ did you know that suffering is limitless/ that horror cannot be circumscribed/ Did you know this/ You who know. (p. 11)

Delbo's images are powerful, frequently drawn from women's everyday pre-camp life and juxtaposed with camp realities: blood on the snow from a slowly dying woman becomes blossoms of "discolored sea anemone" (p. 19). Women lying dead in the snow have become like "dummies" for store windows—stripped of any humanity (pp. 17–19). In passing through the city of Auschwitz, the inhabitants are faceless and take no note of the prisoners: "We had walked through like a wave of morning sickness" (p. 88). Delbo invites me to stand with her at an early morning roll call in the middle of winter:

> I do not look at the stars. They stab with cold. I do not look at the barbed-wire enclosures, white in the night under the lights. They are claws of cold. I see my mother with that mask of hardened will her face has become. My mother. Far. I look at nothing. I think of nothing. (p. 64)

Delbo and Amery speak of emotions, but in very different ways. For Amery, emotions are the passion of the intellect–a means to fulfill its tasks: "Emotions? For all I care, yes. Where is it decreed that enlightenment must be free of emotion? To me the opposite seems to be true. Enlightenment can properly fulfill its task only if it sets to work with passion" (p. xxi). He expresses his ideal in describing fellow prisoners committed to the ideologies of Marxism or Christianity. "I did not want to be one with my believing comrades, but I would have wished to be like them: unshakable, calm, strong" (p. 14).

Numb to all feeling, Amery anesthetizes himself to physical sensation. He distrusts his senses. After eating a plate of sweetened grits, he is euphoric, but the mood cannot last. "Like all intoxications they left behind a dreary, hangover-like feeling of emptiness and shame. They were thoroughly false and are poor proof of the value of the spirit" (pp. 9-10). In the final analysis, Amery deeply distrusts his own emotions. The intellectual, he says, is immune to self-pity. "We don't believe in tears" (p. 68).

For Delbo, emotions are overt, immediate and expressed within contexts of friendship and trust. In the inhuman world of Auschwitz, allowing another to cry in safety is a great gift. In a moving passage, Delbo tells Lulu, another prisoner: "I'm telling you I can't take it any more. This time it's true." Lulu takes Delbo's shovel, shields her from the sight of guards, and allows her to cry:

> I did not wish to cry, but the tears well up and stream down my cheeks. I let them flow, and when one of them touches my lips, I taste the salt and I continue weeping . . . Occasionally [Lulu] turns around and with her sleeve, softly, wipes my face. I keep on crying. I'm not thinking of anything. I just cry. (p. 105)

Drawing from a universal image of maternal love, she concludes, "It is as though I had wept against my mother's breast" (p. 105).

For both Delbo and Amery, memories and images of home are powerful metaphors for what they have lost. For Amery, there is no longer any home, and "the realization that there is no return" leads logically and emotively to the conclusion that "there is no 'new home'. . . . [and] Whoever has lost it remains lost himself" (p. 48). Amery longs for home, but does not write of rebuilding–

even temporarily in his imagination—what he has lost. Auschwitz is unequivocally a story of unredeemable loss—home, country, language, cultural heritage, dignity, past, identity. His intellect ostracizes him from other prisoners and earns him the hatred of the Nazis and Kapos. He is and always will be homeless in the deepest sense possible.

But for Delbo, there remains a present-tense possibility of recreating a home. One spring day, the women seek refuge from the open fields during a rainstorm, and recast the house as a cozy refuge. She writes lovingly of the house as the women imaginatively transform it into a home:

> The house bedecks itself with all its comfortable, familiar pieces of furniture, polished by time. . . . We are huddled against one another . . . The house has grown warm, lived in. . . We look at the rain, hoping it will last till evening. (pp. 77–78)

In their minds the women together create images of what it means to them to be part of humanity.

Fania Fenelon and Szymon Laks

Fania Fenelon and Szymon Laks were members of the Auschwitz II orchestras. Their central theme is the juxtaposition of music and death at Auschwitz. Of the three pairs, Fenelon and Laks most clearly exemplify generalized conclusions about contrasts between women and men at Auschwitz. Laks writes of two instrumental goals: personal survival and musical quality, with the latter taking precedence. For Fenelon, music is not a detached aesthetic; it is unavoidably relational. For her, exploited musicians and love of music cannot co-exist. At Auschwitz, music is tainted, false.

Fenelon meets Clara, a fellow musician, on the train to Auschwitz, and feels a maternal wish to feed and protect her, to take her "under one's wing" (p. 15): "I offered her some of my treasures: sardines, real ones in oil, sausage, pare de campagne, a Camembert, some jam. She gave me some foie gras and champagne . . . we swore never to leave one another, to share everything" (p. 13). They believe that their friendship is stronger than Auschwitz.

Fenelon tells of her introduction to and audition for the women's orchestra at Auschwitz:

"Madame Butterfly!"

Someone was calling Madame Butterfly—in Auschwitz, January 23, 1944, in the quarantine block. Impossible! I scanned the endless rows of gloomy, stinking, three-pieced *cojas*. On each tier, six or more women were packed head to tail like sardines, shaven and virtually naked, shivering with cold and hunger. I'd just been told that there were a thousand women in this barracks, despite the "*Ruhe! Ruhe*"—Silence!—bellowed by the blokowa, our block supervisor, you had to shout to make yourself heard. So Madame Butterfly was somewhat incongruous.

I'd just had a beating in connection with a bucket of dirty water I'd emptied outside, which wasn't allowed. But what was? Tears of rage, mingled with blood, trailed down my grubby cheeks. I wiped the tears away with the back of my hand and huddled up against Clara, whose warmth afforded some comfort. I closed my eyes, and incredibly, it began again: in the midst of the babel a Polish woman was shrieking for Madame Butterfly.

"What's she saying?" I asked my neighbors.

"She's looking for musicians."

"What for?"

"For the orchestra."

"*What* did you say?" I *insisted.*

"The orchestra. Now let it drop, what does it matter to you?"

"But I can play the piano," I protested, "and sing *Madame Butterfly*. I studied with Germaine Martinelli."

"Well, go and tell her."

I leant over, gesticulating; she had to see me. It was forbidden, but I decided to climb down.

Clara held me back. "They're getting at you, it's a joke. You'll get another thrashing."

"Too bad, I'm going anyway."

The girls helped me down. In a fog, aching all over, I hobbled in the direction of the mammoth creature standing in front of the door. A veritable mountain. She stared at me suspiciously: I was so small, so dirty, spattered with mud and blood. She asked loudly, in harsh, bad German: "You, Madame Butterfly?"

"Yes! Yes!"

It seemed that I didn't correspond to this leviathan's idea of a singer, if indeed she had any such Platonic image. She barked something incomprehensible at me. I was steeling myself for another beating, when a girl's voice translated from a lower tier of a *coja*: "She says follow her. One of the French girls in the orchestra recognized you and the *kapo* told her to come and get you."

The impossible was happening. As I followed close on the heels of this mound of flesh I thought in amazement that this could not

logically be the outcome of the horror sequences I'd just lived
through. (pp. 9–11)

Fenelon follows the Polish woman for her audition.

> The Polish woman opened the door and I entered something
> closely resembling paradise. There was light, and a stove; indeed
> it was so warm that I could hardly breathe and stood rooted to the
> spot. Stands, music, a woman on a platform. In front of me pretty
> girls were sitting, well-dressed, with pleated skirts and jerseys,
> holding musical instruments: violins, mandolins, guitars, flutes, pipes
> . . . and a grand piano lording it over them all. . . . A fair girl with
> a gentle face came towards me, with a sympathetic hand she wiped
> away the blood which had run from my mouth and nose, cleaned
> my face with a damp cloth. Angels are wonderful. . . .
>
> Then the picture became animated: the conductor, a tall dark-
> haired woman, dignified and straight-backed, addressed me in
> precise French with a German accent. "Do you play the piano?"
>
> My "Yes, madame" was uttered with such fervor that it rang
> out like an alleluia in a cathedral.
>
> "Well then, go to the piano and accompany yourself to *Ma-
> dame Butterfly*."
>
> Barefoot, I went over to the piano. It was a Bechstein, the dream
> of my life. I climbed onto the stool, put my toes on the pedals and
> my hands on the ivory of the keyboard, and they made me blush
> with shame. I wanted to clench my fists, to hide them. It was so
> long since I'd washed them. But it didn't matter; I was there. . . .
>
> Lovingly my hands made the familiar contact with the black
> and white keys, and I broke into *Un bel di*. Was Puccini going to
> save my life? Then I sang in German *Wenn es Fruhling wird* ("When
> Spring Comes") by Peter Krueder, its rhythm reminiscent of cer-
> tain Gypsy dances.
>
> My hands stopped moving but I kept them on the keyboard;
> as long as they were in contact with it, nothing could happen to
> me. I caressed the piano; it was my savior, my love, my life. Against
> a background of pregnant silence the verdict fell in German:
>
> "*Ja, gut!*"
>
> Then a little more informatively, in French: "I'll have you in
> the orchestra." (pp. 26–27)

True to her promise that they would stay together, Fenelon remembers her friend:

> And Clara? I couldn't abandon her. I'd almost forgotten my
> promise. My exaltation made me incautious and I ventured,

"Madame, madame, I've got a friend, Clara, who's got a marvelous voice. I must go and get her. . . I won't stay here without her. I'll leave, I'll go back over there. . ."

I simply didn't realize what I was saying or the extent of my foolhardiness. For me, a *Nein* would have meant the end of this world. (pp. 27–28)

But the conductor acquiesces, and Clara is brought in for an audition. Clara sings, and Fenelon accompanies her:

And I saw Clara enter, my Clara waddling like a duck, flabby and fat, so fat. Her physical appearance didn't concern the conductor, she barely seemed to notice it. What she wanted was a voice, and that Clara had: a positive nightingale, a light soprano, marvelous, rare. Accompanying her, I had no fears, and rightly.

"I'll have you. I want you both in the orchestra. I'll tell our chief of camp straight away and get you dressed." (p. 28)

Laks' audition for the men's Auschwitz orchestra follows a different line. It is up to him to promote his own musical talents, not to musicians, but to a group of bridge players. Laks tells of the steps leading up to his audition for the orchestra as "the first miracle in a long series of miracles that kept me alive and ultimately restored my freedom" (p. 31). He tells of a "savior," a benefactor in the form of a barracks chief and refuses to name him, but offers the chief a blessing: "If he is still alive, may the rest of his life pass 'as on a broad field, sweetly and happily.' And if he is not alive, may the soil over him be light" (p. 32). In the following passage Laks credits an authority in Auschwitz (apparently a highly ranked prisoner) and himself with his privileges, and offers a minor role to luck:

Tall, broad-shouldered, a real athlete, he stood as though on purpose beside my bunk and in a stentorian voice called out in Polish, "Is there someone here who speaks Polish and plays bridge?"

I almost failed to understand what he meant, but instinctively I stopped munching on my bread, jumped down from the bunk, and stood before him at attention.

"Come on!"

There were no other candidates. As I learned later, my transport, which had come from France, included very few people who spoke Polish. So to some extent I was Fortune's darling.

A few minutes later, dirty, unshaven, not believing my eyes and ears, I was sitting at a bridge table in the private room of the barracks chief, in the company of two other VIPs in striped clothing, and playing one rubber after another like an equal with equals. . . .

During one of the hands we played, I managed to mutter to him [the barracks chief] that I was a violinist and composer. He looked at me with a bitter, honest reproach.

"Why didn't you tell me this sooner? Tomorrow you'll stay in the barracks and I'll take you over to the orchestra."

A second companion added, choking with laughter, "And if you're accepted, maybe you'll live a little longer, ha, ha, ha!"

All three of them burst out laughing. Their merriment very nearly spread to me.

My benefactor did more for me than he promised. After the card game was over, he gave me a haircut and shave, had me wash up in a bowl of the hot concoction that had been served to us as "tea," and told me to report to him at dawn on the following day.

The very thought that tomorrow I would not leave the camp for work filled me with good cheer such as I had not known for a long time. (pp. 30–32)

The next morning, Laks arrives at Barracks 15 for his audition. Like Fenelon, he is immediately awed by the instruments, but it draws him closer to the camp elite, and he offers a more detailed description of the instruments soon to be at his disposal:

My attention was first attracted, "professionally" one might say, by the wooden partition a few meters away on which were hanging all sorts of brass and woodwind instruments, everything polished to a bright shine. I distinguished in turn a huge tuba helicon, a trombone, a few trumpets, a brass tenor and alto horns, saxophones, clarinets, and two flutes, one a piccolo. Leaning against the wall in one of the corners was an impressive double bass with a bow stuck under the strings, in another a bass drum with cymbals and a snare drum with all of the percussion paraphernalia. On a wide, solid shelf specifically designed for this purpose were a few accordions and violins in cases. One of them, somewhat bigger than the others, probably contained a viola. I failed to see a violoncello. A second shelf, somewhat smaller, was filled with music scores and a pile of blank music paper. . . .

My angel-bridge player, who had conducted me here, walked up to the older man [sitting eating breakfast] and, pointing to me, whispered something in his ear. He was unquestionably the conductor of the orchestra and had an engaging appearance, with kind-hearted eyes. At first he took me for a Frenchman, since he knew that my transport had come from France, but before long his face lit up when he learned that I was "really" a Pole and that he could speak to me in Polish. He gave me a violin and asked me to play something.

My fingers were stiff, bruised, my arms sore, the bow slipped out of my hand, but fortunately my left arm was almost sound. I thought it best to play something technically effective and, without reflection, I rushed into the first bars of Mendelssohn's concerto, completely forgetting that he was a Jewish composer and that the performance of his works was forbidden in Germany and in the occupied countries as well. Quite fortunately, after only a few bars the conductor gave me a sign to stop.

"Good. Technique not bad, not bad. Tell your barracks chief that you have been accepted and for him to transfer you to this barracks." (pp. 32–34)

After a week in the orchestra, in dual roles of musician and field worker, Laks is promoted to music copyist. He no longer works in the fields, and his musical career at Auschwitz advances steadily. His first step is to become acting director of the orchestra. When the official conductor Zaborski dies, in November 1942, Laks' nemesis Kopka "did not hesitate to take advantage of the situation and imperiously nominated himself *Kapellmeister*" (p. 45). Laks is not to be outdone:

the real responsibility for the orchestra fell on Zuk[6] and me, with the tacit consent of Kopka. (p. 44)

Kopka was directing, but:

. . . the rehearsals were now taking place under my direction. . . . Kopka kept handing the conductor's baton over to me. The truth of the matter was—I admit it without any scruples—that I had intentionally introduced into my orchestrations the greatest number of difficulties in rhythm, counterpoint, and syncopation, for the percussion instruments as well, which made it impossible for Kopka to conduct the rehearsals, let alone public performances! I have never regretted the use of this dirty trick. (p. 55)

After some time, Kopka falls into disfavor. He becomes ill and is to be sent to the front:

. . . he [Kopka] had to step down from the pedestal of being a well-off *Kapellmeister* to the status of an ordinary private, condemned in advance to hunger, cold, maybe even death. . . . This made me the real, though unofficial, conductor of the orchestra, which now numbered forty musicians. I could work in peace and enrich the repertoire either on my own initiative or at the instructions of the commander and his subordinates. I could also conduct rehearsals and public performances as I liked, without the amateurish meddling of the titular *Kapellmeister*. (p. 60)

Unexpectedly, Kopka returns "at the most inconvenient moment" (p. 62), and overhears the orchestra practicing "forbidden Polish music in the barracks" (p. 63). Kopka reports Laks to the commander, who in turn officially dismisses the *Kapellmeister* from his post:

> The commander got up from behind his desk, walked up to Kopka, and gave him two slaps in the face. And now something completely unbelievable happened! *Lagerfuhrer* Schwarzhuber tore off the band with the silver lyre from Kopka's arm and, looking him straight in the eye, shouted in anger, "Du Lump! Dy Schwein! Raus! (You wretch! You pig! Get out!)"
>
> After which, turning to me, he handed me the shreds of the armband and said gently, almost kindly, "Und jetzt nenne Ich Sie Lagerkapellmeister (and now I appoint you Kapellmeister)!"
>
> For Kopka two slaps and addressed as "du"; for me the office of *Kapellmeister* and addressed politely as "Sie" . . . all-powerful music! (pp. 63–64)

Laks' instrumental ability for self-promotion extends beyond music. He becomes a secretary and translator for an officer, Albert Haemmerle, a barracks chief who "had raised the art of dispassionate murder to the greatest heights" (p. 68), and a courier between Haemmerle and his young male lover, Bolek. It was a relationship which "did not last long, but even its brevity turned out to be highly profitable. . . . each time I played the secretary, I emerged loaded down with generous gifts" (pp. 68, 69).

True to his stated purpose, Laks gives us information about the structure of orchestras in the Nazi concentration camps:

> The first ambition of the *Lagerfuhrer* (commander) of every camp worthy of the name was to form his own *Lagerkapelle* (camp musical group), whose main role was to ensure the flawless functioning of camp discipline and on occasion to afford our guardian angels a bit of entertainment and relaxation, so necessary in carrying out their not always appreciated work. . . .
>
> In Auschwitz I . . . this proto-Auschwitz, which had been established in June 1940, a large orchestra had existed for quite some time under the direction of Franz Nierychlo. (pp. 17, 41)

Fenelon and Laks do not live in isolation.[7] Through their music, both created or were absorbed into networks: Fenelon's within a more private world with other prisoners in the women's orchestra, and Laks, all too often, with the powerful and official world of the SS.

Fenelon's ties follow less official channels. Like Nomberg-Przytyk, she tells collective stories through the words of others, often drawing from female imagery: "we learned the story . . . gradually, piecing together a patchwork of whispered information" (p. 167). Other women tell their personal stories, and explain the workings of Auschwitz–beatings, selections and killings. Much of what Fenelon learns about Auschwitz comes through what other musicians tell her. Fenelon writes that Little Irene, a mediocre violinist and an idealistic Marxist, talks compulsively about the workings of Auschwitz:

> I'd survived the selection of my arrival, but I didn't know what the criteria were, or how other selections took place. I wanted to ask, but kept a feeble silence. However, Irene talked on, perhaps wanting to unburden herself of the horror that was stifling her. One had to be new here to agree to listen to her.
> "I think that the selections carried out on those who aren't new arrivals are the worst. . . . The trucks arrive, stop in front of the blocks. Inside, a safe distance from the foul smell, the SS point out those selected: the thinnest, the shivering, the sick who try and hide, the girls who are disliked by the blockowa, the *kapo*, the kitchen girl. . . why not? And they're brought out with blows from rifle butts, clubbed, kicked, punched, butted. The blockowas, egged on by the SS, are the worst; they lash out the most of all. Some women shriek and fight. I saw one throw herself at an SS man, nails clawing his face; he clubbed her down, and everyone was forced to walk over her body, still living, just one mass of red . . ." (p. 59)

Fenelon passes these stories on to us, with a warning, "I wished she'd stop. I didn't want to hear any more. But Irene continued, and I could only hope it was therapeutic" (p. 59).

Fenelon's reaction when other women confide in her their physical attraction to other women in the orchestra is one of loving encouragement:

> It was perfectly clear: Marta was in love with Little Irene. . . .
> In Birkenau, one couldn't long remain ignorant of homosexuality–

it was rife; it offered the women satisfaction for their fantasies, allayed their solitude, their sexual needs. If, for many, it was just a way of cheating reality, for some it was a revelation, and Marta was possibly one of those. (pp. 144–45)

Marta tells Fania:

"Oh, Fania, it's not possible!"
"Of course it is, and it's no disaster." And I explained to her that to the pure all is pure, she so needed reassurance.
"So, Fania, it's not wrong to love as I do?"
"In the camp one might call it a blessing."
"Thank you. You've done me so much good."
Was it wrong to love here? If I believed in God, I would say that to feel a pure, clean feeling in this place, where Evil reigned supreme, was a sign of His blessing. Loving wasn't wrong, it just seemed amazing to be able to isolate oneself sufficiently for it. The camp had entirely sterilized the need in me, and I wondered desperately whether it would ever return. (p. 147)

For most of the women in the orchestra, their fears are collective fears. They would live or die together; their musical skills and the whims of the SS were all that stood between them and the gas chambers. The women discuss a new commander of the crematoria: "We'll have to play well for him. No wrong notes" (p. 229). As an anonymous mass of musicians, they exist only so long as they meet the needs of the SS. Not only music, but—in a vein similar to Delbo—other arts bind them together:

As usual, Ewa and I had been reciting poetry to one another: it was our way of keeping in contact with the other world. Florette, chin on knees, Anny and Big Irene had listened to us. . . . I had told them an installment of the *Picture of Dorian Gray*; each evening, from memory, I "read" them a chapter before they went to bed. (p. 141)

While both Fenelon and Laks write of music and interaction with prisoners as a form of relaxation for the Germans, their stories differ markedly in the implications this has for the prisoners. For Laks, this is a time of sharing in a common humanity and love of culture. For Fenelon, these times emphasize and widen the chasm between herself and her captors. Her descriptions of the women's orchestra have a sexual subtext of objectification and degradation. They "have to get all tarted up" (p. 95) to play their Sunday afternoon concerts for the SS. The SS commanded the women of the orchestra to transcribe and compose scores, play marches as prisoners went to and from work, and perform private concerts for them in the evening–an activity she describes as "nightwork" (p. 55). She sings on command for the SS with simulated passion and hidden disgust, and describes the scene:

> For me, singing was a free act, and I was not free; it was above all a way of giving pleasure, giving love, and I felt a frantic desire to see those three SS men stuck like pigs, right here, at my feet. Standing in front of those men with their buttocks spread out over their chairs. (p. 93)

She continues, and her language shifts: she is no longer standing, singing and fantasizing revenge. She is lying down, completely vulnerable:

> I felt as though I were living through one of those nightmares in which you want to cry out and can't. That cry would save your life, enable you to escape from the attendant horrors, and yet you lie there open-mouthed with no lifesaving sound emerging. . . . Suddenly I had a vision of the night clubs where I used to sing. Admittedly they were crammed with Germans, a positive mass of grey-green, but I was there of my own accord, willingly; singing was a cover, I was there only to deceive the better. (pp. 93–94)

She writes of "the concerts which the SS came to, at times chosen by themselves, to relax after their 'hard' work" (p. 55). After a day of sending thousands of deportees to their deaths [in the gas chambers] "they go back into their mess to have a quiet drink, play the piano, have a girl . . . or they come here to listen to music" (p. 60).

One evening, after a hard day at the ramp, the brutal Herr Lagerfuhrer Kramer and two other SS men demand, "Now, a moment's respite for all of us. We are going to hear some music" (p. 92). The orchestra plays Schumann's "Reverie" and Fenelon sings "Madame Butterfly." The SS, particularly Kramer, are "appropriately" moved. The music "washes over him." Not without bitter irony, Fenelon observes, "[s]atisfied, he had relieved himself of his 'selection' by listening to music as others might do by masturbating. Relaxed, the Lagerfuhrer shook his head and expressed his pleasure. . . . 'How beautiful, how moving!'" (pp. 92–93).

For Fenelon, her disgust at singing for the SS is not limited to performing for male audiences:

> Maria Mandel [a German Jewish prisoner] was the perfect representative of the young German woman depicted in propaganda. She had a lovely Dietrich voice, guttural in the lower register. She pointed to me: "I'd like *meine kleine Sangerin* to sing *Madame Butterfly* in German." . . . Mandel had removed her cape and sat down, looking dreamy. Could it be that she regarded herself as a sentimental geisha? I hated myself at the thought of giving her pleasure. . . . This was the worst moment, the time when it was difficult not to give up. Despite all the wise lectures I gave myself, having entertained that SS woman after a selection filled me with the utmost disgust. (pp. 61, 62, 63)

Laks, by contrast, identifies with the Germans in their appreciation of music. He praises the Germans' appreciation of music: "There really is no doubt that Germans are music lovers from birth and that nothing musical is alien to them. Their insistence on having music at a place like Auschwitz is only one example of this passion" (p. 69).

Musical taste and talent are the primary bases on which Laks makes personal judgments—of prisoners and of Germans. A German who loves music of a certain quality is, to Laks—at some level—a better, more sympathetic, German. He speaks warmly of the young Rottenfuhrer Pery Broad, "the most faithful friend of our orchestra" (p. 79). At Broad's trial after the war, Laks writes, "There was a lot of talk about the numerous crimes committed by this whippersnapper. As far as I know, though, no one mentioned his uncommon musical talents" (p. 80).

Laks concludes that, when one of the SS listened to music, "he somehow became strangely similar to a human being. His voice lost its typical harshness, he suddenly acquired an easy manner, and one could talk with him almost as one equal to another. . . . At such moments," Laks concludes, "the hope stirred in us that maybe everything was not lost after all" (p. 70).

Laks places his concern for his fellow musicians within a context of concern for the quality of music. He arranges for orchestra members to obtain indoor work, not to save their lives but to enhance the music and "enable them to retain the nimbleness of their hands and fingers and thereby ensure a better sound and a more rhythmic cadence of the marches" (p. 66). He does not want them to go hungry because "a well-fed musician plays better than a hungry one" (p. 97). Laks' problem, the orchestra's problem, is that musicians died:

> . . . causing empty spaces in the chords, quite often in solo parts. This imposed on me the gloomy obligation of carefully observing the physical and mental health of my less hardy colleagues. I was also forced to make use of a special kind of orchestration, called *odeon* in musical slang, which makes it possible for any group to perform any work, regardless of the presence or absence of one or even a few musicians. This is achieved by writing the most important themes in small notes in the other parts, so that if the main soloist is absent he can be replaced by someone else who plays these small notes instead. In time I gained real mastery in this strange art. (p. 48)

In Laks' story, music often takes precedence over all else. When the Czech camp of four thousand, including its orchestra, is murdered one day, Laks and his orchestra inherit their music stands and instruments. "We also inherited from the Czechs a few violins, a trumpet, and a priceless violoncello, whose lack I had painfully felt. Not only would it enrich the sound of our orchestra, but it would give me the opportunity of forming a string quartet" (p. 91).

In Fenelon's story, music is a metaphor for life. Her story is in many respects a restitution narrative: liberation brings her the freedom to sing with her heart, and revives her life. She begins the first chapter of her story of Auschwitz with closure—a dramatic story of liberation which reassures the reader with its themes of rebirth:

> The girls, those girls of whom I'd grown so fond, threw themselves at me, shaking me. "Fania, wake up! Do you hear, the English are here. You must speak to them." . . .
> "Sing, Fania, sing!" someone shrieked. The order galvanized me; I opened my mouth desperately. The soldier thought I was at my last gasp. . . I started on the first verse of the *Marseillaise*. My voice had not died; I was alive. . . . The air hit me like a slap. I

choked and was reborn. The girls ran out behind us. Technically no doubt I still had typhus, but the moment I found the strength to sing, I felt I'd recovered. . . . Someone handed me a microphone. . . . I sang the *Marseillaise* again. . . . The microphone holder insisted: "Please, miss, it's for the BBC."

I sang "God Save the King," and tears filled the British soldiers' eyes.

I sang the *Internationale* and the Russian deportees joined in.

I sang, and in front of me, around me, from all corners of the camp, creeping along the sides of the shacks, dying shadows and skeletons stirred, rose up, grew taller. A great "Hurrah" burst forth and swept along like a breaker, carrying all before it. They had become men and women once again. (pp. 6–9)

Fenelon frames her entire story with restitution themes, and ends with a story of new life:

We sat up firmly and began to look life in the eye. For some of us, it was like a rebirth. . . when the sun was less hot, we got up and calmly, hand in hand, we took the path back.

On this path, coming towards us, was a group of Serbs, brown curls, dark eyes, white teeth chewing grass, a flower, shirts open on sunburnt skin, warm skin one wanted to touch. . . .

We felt ourselves becoming light—and young, so young. The young men laughed like conquerors. We wanted to flirt, to go off with them arm in arm for an hour, a day, a lifetime. . .

We were saved. (p. 260)

Fenelon's final chapter, "What Became of Us," resonates with themes of restoration—family, courage, and fulfillment—following liberation:

Life was out there waiting for us; we threw ourselves into it and it carried us along, some of us farther than others. . . . Elsa, patient, calm, and self-effacing, wasn't able to bear the joy of return; she died shortly after our liberation.

Little Irene did have the time to marry—not her Paul, but someone else. . . .

Ewa the Polish girl, my great friend, returned to her son and husband. And when I saw her again in 1960, she had become director of a theatre in Krakow, just as she'd hoped.

Big Irene married on her return to Belgium. She has two children and lives in Brussels, not far from Anny, who is an active business woman, also married and the mother of two children.

Florette had a number of difficulties which she faced with courage, and finally married too. She has two children and a business somewhere in the south of France.

Maria has managed her life perfectly; married to the man she always loved–and who was one of the rare men to wait–she has an important post in the Prefecture de la Seine.

I learned by chance in 1958 that Ewa the Hungarian had married and was living in Switzerland, and that her compatriot Lili was living in London with an English husband. (pp. 261–62)

REPRISE AND REFLECTIONS

True, I had found comforting motifs in women's Auschwitz stories. Each of these three women speak of the wisdom of sister-hood, of returning to society to tell their truths, of restitution of belief in some human beings. But perhaps the appeal of arguments that women "made better survivors" than men in Auschwitz, and that men survived "better" when they adopted female-style patterns of mutual support, reflects my desires for comforting or inspiring stories? Had I looked for something, anything, that suggests agency in the face of genocide? Did I long for hints that even the worst that humans can do to other humans can be overcome, if not through force, then through mutual support and caring?

While my first reading centers on patterns of gendered differ-ences that can be found in Auschwitz survivor stories, it is equally important that we not valorize the women's experiences. The Holocaust "is a story of loss," writes Pawelczynska, "not gain" (1979, p. 757). And nothing, including gender, can honestly turn the collective stories of those who were there into stories of collective betterment, growth, or gain.

This first reading and some of the earliest Holocaust studies of women's stories are a necessary first step in countering total-izing ideology, true to much of what I found in Auschwitz stories, and products of a particular historical moment. This step echoes more general feminist literature on life writing from the 1970s, as described by Nancy K. Miller, contrasted women's story-telling with that of men:

> To a great extent, this assumption of a universal female subject was of course a sign of the times. . . . Challenging the universality of the male autobiographical subject–the universal, but as it turned out Western, European, heterosexual, in a word, canonical 'I'– seemed an all-consuming task; the Female Subject was his

> counterpart and adversary. . . . [The] appeal for a discourse articulating the diversity of situated, delineated, unevenly developed female subjects was not to find an echo in mainstream feminist literary studies for a while. (1991, p. 125)

All stories, female or male, purportedly objective or not, are structured by gendered themes and relative positions of power and knowledge (Benhabib 1988; Benstock 1988; Fraser 1989; Miller 1991; Personal Narratives Group 1987; Smith 1987). But gender is not unequivocally the singular constitutional determinant of these stories. Gender permeates, inflects, and informs—rather than determines—stories, and must be contextualized along with factors such as ethnicity, social class, nationality, and ideology, and individual personality. Each complicates the other. As I worked my way through layers of stories, I found differences based on nationality, the hierarchies of Auschwitz, and what survivors simply call "luck." As Primo Levi tells us, without enormous luck, it was impossible to survive Auschwitz. In his last work, *The Drowned and the Saved,* he concludes: "The worst survived, that is, the fittest; the best all died" (1988, p. 82).

Chapter Four is a story of my second reading. In it I tell of reading through an expanded template, categorizing storied particularities that, while informed by gender, are not determined by it. This story tells how survivors clung to or created frameworks and categories by which they tried to recognize—or at least locate—themselves and others in the brutal chaos of Auschwitz.

NOTES

1. Langer's analysis is most thorough, focusing on lesser-known survivors such as Delbo, as well as the better known ones such as Wiesel.

2. The conference was organized by Joan Ringelheim and sponsored by The Institute for Research in History in New York City. See Katz and Ringelheim (1983) for conference proceedings.

3. In a conversation with Sybil Milton in the summer of 1994, she noted that gender effects were much more complex and multifaceted during the Holocaust than previously thought.

4. As Nancy K. Miller argues, "When we return to male-authored texts in the light of patterns found in female-authored texts—reading *for*

connection, for the relations to the other—we may want to revise the canonical views of male autobiographical identity altogether" (1994, p. 5).

5. See Camilla Stivers for a discussion of the importance of women telling their own stories: "Having rejected women's historical status as the object of the male subject's defining gaze, feminism demands that those who have been objectified now be able to define themselves, to tell their own stories. This is essentially a claim that each human being occupies a legitimate position from which to experience, interpret, and constitute the world" (1993, p. 411).

6. Ludwik Zuk-Skarszewski, a "violinist, clarinetist, copyist-arranger" (p. 36) in the men's orchestra at Birkenau, and a close friend of Laks.

7. Neither Fenelon nor Laks cites the other's work. Laks writes in his "Overture" to *Music of Another World*, "As far as I know, there is no book discussing in detail the real role of music in the life of the camps" (1989, pp. 5–6).

CHAPTER 4
Situated Voices

The blokowa *would inspect the block, looking straight in front of her. She did not see us at all. She walked with a slow, majestic step, her proud head held high. You would not believe that she was a prisoner, just like the rest of us, and the lowest category of prisoner, at that, a Jew. Once she caught an old woman in front of the block who was apparently unable to reach the toilet, which was a considerable distance from the block. We heard an especially inhuman moaning of a victim being beaten without pity: "Oh you swine! Do you think I'm going to suffer for you? Die!"*

—Sarah Nomberg-Przytyk 1985, p. 21

Journal Entry: April 17, 1995

A new translation of Charlotte Delbo's work is finally available. Rosette Lamont, a woman who knew Delbo and has translated other works of hers, has translated a trilogy, *None of Us Will Return, Useless Knowledge* and *The Measure of Our Days*, now published by Yale University Press as *Auschwitz and After*. Until now, only *None of Us Will Return* has been available in English. Lawrence Langer's ten page introduction begins, "Charlotte Delbo is still little known in this country, and not very well known in her own" (p. ix). I read the entire work in a single day, and begin re-writing my own work.

My first reading of Auschwitz survivors' stories found many examples of gendered differences, and resisted the privilege of any universal voice. This reading, however, glosses over the full diversity of survivors' stories. The more I followed a binary gendered reading, the more inadequate it felt. It reinforced the notion of woman as marginalized "Other" and often failed to account for ways in which survivors portrayed themselves and others. Such a reading ignored survivors' attempts in Auschwitz and in their writings to maintain or re-establish multiple identities for themselves. The stories of Auschwitz are too complex to fit neatly into gender stereotypes. Women as well as men tell of violence and treachery. Gender sets permeable boundaries for experience and narrative, but how it does so is interwoven with other aspects of social reality.

I found it impossible to stay within the confines of a two-dimensional gendered template. Rather, the frame repeatedly slipped aside to reveal other patterns within the fabric of their tales. For while gender permeates these stories, it does not act alone, and does not determine every aspect of the stories. I could not neatly section off portions of content or style—for example inter-personal relationships and narrative closure—and contain them within two-dimensional formations. Although women were doubly oppressed—as prisoners and as women, as Jews and as potential mothers of Jewish children—there is no single story of female experience at Auschwitz. Women, as well as men, tell of multiple identities interacting—nationality, ethnicity, ideology, and status.

I looked again at feminist scholarship on the Holocaust. Heinemann, author of a 1986 book on women's Holocaust writings that I had drawn from in my first reading, also wrote in her earlier (1981) dissertation that women's positions of relative privilege in ghettos and camps greatly influenced the stories they told. I was also drawn again to the reflexive perspectives of Joan Ringelheim. Her unique feminist Holocaust scholarship (1984, 1985, 1990, 1993) pushes the frontiers of feminist and Holocaust studies far beyond two-dimensional templates. Ringelheim turns issues of gender differences around and warns against assuming that women's survival strategies were positive. She argues against a cultural feminist view that looks at individual responses and ignores the context of gender-based oppression surrounding sup-posed strengths of women.[1] Ringelheim challenges me to ques-tion the stories of women survivors, to ask, how does one evaluate survival mechanisms learned through pre-camp oppression? What prices have women paid for their survival? Were friendships and interpersonal ties uniformly positive? Have women survivors transformed their stories in culturally acceptable ways in order to live with themselves in the present—are they in part deceiving themselves when they emphasize friendship as a means of survival? Once aware of these questions I could no longer rest with my first reading.

Valorizing women's stories and experiences that arise out of oppression belies gender and racial tyranny. It tolerates—and even encourages—my hope that there might be satisfactory happy endings for the tiny fraction of individuals who survived, and lets me attribute their survival to resourcefulness and human goodness. Unfortunately, and "[u]ltimately," Ringelheim reminds me, "survival was luck" (1993, p. 383). Gender may have influenced how people survived, but being female did not increase women's chances of survival. In fact, Ringleheim has carefully documented statistics showing that because of Nazi policies, Jewish practices and assumptions, and social organization, more women than men were killed during the Holocaust. Perhaps I was too quick to judge, then, too quick to confuse exploitation with valor, an overwhelming passion for music with purely instrumental rationality.

A closer reading of Auschwitz stories does not allow me to valorize women's oppression. Stories of reliance on networks of family and friends as found in women's personal narratives are tinged with, in the words of the Personal Narratives Group, "women's relative powerlessness, their lack of access to more formal and institutional routes to influence, . . . a survival strategy shared with other relatively powerless groups" (1989, p. 21).

Likewise male prisoners at Auschwitz had neither power nor formal access to authority. It should not be surprising that their writings exhibit characteristics traditionally associated with female authorship (Miller 1994).

In this chapter I tell of reading these stories for a second time, and of hearing discordant voices that challenge my wish to find comfort in survivors' words.

As survivors write of ways by which prisoners located themselves within the social and moral confusion of Auschwitz, they resist the dehumanization that comes with the destruction of personal identity. Resistance and attempts to anchor one's identity take many forms. Survivors' use of literature, so common in the women's stories, helps ground them in their remembered identities. Delbo tries to anchor herself with names and contexts of time. She remembers her date of arrival, January 27, and counts off the days:

> We had taken the trouble to count the days from our arrival on Wednesday the twenty-seventh of January in order to keep track of the dates. What dates? What did it matter whether it was Friday or Saturday, this or that anniversary? The dates we had to remember were those of Yvonne's or Suzanne's death, the death of Rosette or Marcelle. We wanted to be able to say, "So and so died on . . . " when they'd ask us after we returned. . . . On Sunday, the columns did not leave the camp. That provided a point of reference and allowed us to reestablish a correct count when we lost track of the days. (pp. 147–48)

Within the hermetically sealed world of Auschwitz, and in the memories and stories of survivors constructed years and decades later, individuals assert their singularity. Their stories cannot be squeezed into two-dimensional taxonomies. Any reading, Costello reminds me, must "situate gender where it belongs—in a matrix of historical contingencies" (1991, p. 127).

NATIONALITY, ETHNICITY, AND IDEOLOGY

Survivors write of nationality, ethnicity, and ideology strongly shaping prisoners' expectations and experiences. They tell of German Jews, in particular, expecting special treatment because of their (perceived) Teutonic status. Nomberg-Przytyk describes a scene that belies any images we might have of universal sisterhood among the women prisoners at Auschwitz: "'I am German, not Jewish,' one of them, an older woman, kept repeating . . . 'They can't treat us like this.'" The German Jews, Nomberg-Przytyk concludes, "despised [the Polish-Jewish prisoners] their fellow victims, more than they hated the SS" (p. 19).[2]

Fenelon tells of lines of discrimination drawn on the basis of nationality. The women's conductor, Alma Rose—a German Jew and a niece of Gustav Mahler—defined Germans as "the best musicians in the world" (p. 117). Fenelon, a Frenchwoman vying with the Germans for cultural distinction, identifies the Polish women prisoners as most brutal. She tells how, shortly after arriving at Auschwitz, Polish women prisoners roughly shaved her and stripped away her clothes. She promises herself, "If I ever get out of here, I'll kill a Polish woman. And I'll see to it that all the rest die; that shall be my aim in life. I always had to have an aim in life" (p. 19).

Survivors frequently take nationality and ethnicity as their starting points in identifying other prisoners. For Laks, Ludwik Zuk is "Pole" (p. 14). Musicians are "Frenchmen, a few Greeks, Jews from Poland and Germany, but mostly Dutchmen, who turned out to be excellent instrumentalists" (p. 42). Jews and non-Jews receive distinctively different treatment. "Non-Jew had the right to regular correspondence and received food packages" (p. 15). Nomberg-Przytyk writes of the "Jews from Holland" (p. 18), "Poles from Krakow" (p. 111), "Slovak Jews" (p. 38), "Orli. . . a German Communist" (p. 36), a doctor who is "small, young, and unusually beautiful . . . a Czech Jew" (p. 37), "Erika . . . a Jewish girl from Germany" (p. 48), "Mala, a Jewess from Belgium" (p. 100), "Hans, an Austrian comrade" (p. 121), and "a strange girl . . . [who] was not Jewish" (p. 6).

Delbo distinguishes herself from Jewish women who "are shorn every month" (p. 119). For her, the Jewish women are not fully comrades. One Sunday, on a macabre garden-making assignment, the women, transferring loads of dirt in their aprons, are forced to run for hours between rows of bludgeon-wielding Kapos. The Frenchwomen try to run together, protecting each other from the blows. But the Jewish women make this difficult. "[B]elieving they are taking more of a beating, [they] slip in between our striped dresses. . . . They fill us with pity but we do not want to be separated from each other" (p. 92). The Frenchwomen exclude the Jewish women from their circle of protection.

In the same scene, the next paragraph, there is also a Frenchman, a member of the resistance: "We would brave anything to speak to him" (p. 92). For Delbo, the boundaries of kinship are fluid: ideology and nationality take precedence over gender and ethnicity. Polish women, women of the orchestra, Jewish women—none are invariably comrades or kin. Though she was a communist, with expressions of egalitarian humanity, Delbo's judgments of female prisoners are often bound in nationality and ethnicity. There are not only gendered voices; there are nationalized voices, ethnic voices, ideological voices. Delbo tells of times when the ability to speak French often separates the prisoners into "us" and the "others": "There I was in the midst of unknown faces. Russian women, Polish women, no one I recalled ever seeing before, no one who spoke French" (p. 193).

Delbo tells of a time when she is faint with thirst and a Polish woman offers her water and asks, "'Chelba?'. . . I have no bread. I give away all my bread in the evening for a bit of tea. I answer that I have no bread, pleading with my lips. She upsets the tin cup and the water spills [to the ground]" (p. 74).

The national lines along which distinctions are made change from one circumstance to another. On Christmas Eve, the women plan an elaborate feast and Christmas party. Delbo tells of a time when she and her friends trade bread to the Russian women in exchange for onions to make a sauce for their potatoes, but exclude them from their celebration: "We meant to celebrate a traditional Christmas. A Polish Christmas, since there was a larger contingent of Polish women. The Russians, also numerous, were not invited" (p. 162).

Fenelon and Delbo do not define all other women prisoners as sisters, and the Polish women are categorically unaccepted. Social integration and regulation of conflict belong within the confines of a particular group. Delbo writes of "no one . . . no one from our group, I mean" (p. 148), and explains that "you cannot survive without the others. By 'others' we meant those members of our group who hold you up, or carry you when you can no longer walk, those who help you hold fast when you're at the end of your rope" (p. 193).

What is selflessness, and what is calculated instrumental rationality? Most pointedly in Levi's work, these questions do not have clear-cut answers. Levi remembers with painful clarity that when he found a rare supply of water, he shared it only with his close friend Alberto. He speaks of "belated shame" (1988, p. 81) for this "selfishness extended to the person closest to you" (1988, p. 80). Levi has constructed a mutually supportive family in Auschwitz. Alberto was kin and entitled to a share in the treasure of pure water. The other prisoners were not: "Daniele had caught a glimpse of us in the strange position, supine near the wall among the rubble . . . and then had guessed" (1988, p. 80).[3]

For some survivors, ideology is central to identity at Auschwitz. Amery writes of political and religious ideology as a source of strength for prisoners themselves:

> I must confess that I felt, and still feel, great admiration for both my religiously and politically committed comrades. . . . One way or the other, in the decisive moments their political or religious belief was an inestimable help to them, while we skeptical and humanistic intellectuals took recourse, in vain, to our literary, philosophical, and artistic household gods. . . their belief or their ideology gave them that firm foothold in the world from which they spiritually unhinged the SS state. . . . They survived better or died with more dignity than their irreligious or unpolitical intellectual comrades, who often were infinitely better educated and more practiced in exact thinking. (pp. 12–13)

Sara Nomberg-Przytyk clearly outlines her position at Auschwitz. She tells how, shortly after her arrival at the camp, she narrowly escaped death in the gas chambers because of her connections with other communists in the camp. As she tells it, she and Sonia had been political prisoners together in the Fordonia prison from 1938–1939 and again in the Bialystok Ghetto. In the Bialystok Ghetto, both had "joined the Jewish anti-Hitler volunteer army" (p. 23). Sonia had been sent to Auschwitz about a year before Nomberg-Przytyk. The two friends meet there about a week after Nomberg-Przytyk's arrival, when she has decided that suicide would be preferable to camp existence. Sonia, dressed in warm clothes, recognizes Nomberg-Przytyk:

> "Don't torment yourself," Sonia whispered in my ear. "We will have you out of here by tomorrow. We will 'organize' a warm sweater and boots for you. I will bring food for you. Do you know why I came here? To find friends and help them as much as we can. There are many of our people in the camp"—meaning international anti-Hitler organization. "We are not without our means, even in this hell. . . . Things will be different tomorrow." (pp. 24–25)

But tomorrow only brings selection, and Nomberg-Przytyk assumes, "I knew that for me selection meant death" (p. 24). She stands in line, waiting for her turn in the gas chambers:

> Suddenly a young girl appeared in front of me. Dressed in a sports coat, with a hood on her head, she went down the line asking, in a hushed voice, "Who is a friend of Sonia?" I became proud. Could they mean me? "That's me," I said, not completely sure that they really meant me.
>
> She looked at me quickly, as though she could read me completely with this one look. That is how people looked at each other in Auschwitz, as though they undressed each other with a glance. "Come with me," she whispered. "How can I?" I replied. "The *sztubowe.*" I was afraid of their blows. "Don't ask," she said. "Just come." I stepped out of the line. The hands of the *sztubowe* parted before my guide. We stepped outside the chain that surrounded the people condemned to death. Eva (that was the stranger's name) led me along a narrow path. She took me to the rear of the bath house, where those who had lived through the selection were waiting. I was saved. (p. 27)

A *schreiberka* or clerk sends Nomberg-Przytyk to the infirmary to hide for three days. Marusia, a nurse, and Mancy, a physician, introduce themselves and assign Nomberg-Przytyk to a position of relative safety for the remainder of her time at Auschwitz.

> "We are Czech Communists. We know all about you. You will work with us in the infirmary as a clerk. You will only sleep on the block. Early in the morning, before roll call, you will come here to us and will work with us." Marusia spoke very fast and with a smile. It was obvious that she was trying to convince herself that the matter was well taken care of, and that everything would come out well. Mancy was quiet. . . .
>
> Officially, I was supposed to be sick. According to my sick card I belonged in the hospital, but in actuality I was supposed to work in the infirmary. Mancy tried to ease my anxieties by telling me that there are many functionaries on the block who, like me, were posing as patients. They felt safe because, on the block, selections were made only during the daytime hours, and at that time the functionaries were not among the sick. (p. 38)

Religious and political fervor also divide and are, at times, a source of irritation to others. In a rare comment on religious life in the camps, Amery reflects:

> As soon as I got to know them, their fanaticism irritated me.
> Despite the reality that surrounded them, they continued to be-
> lieve in the glory of the Chosen People. Here in Auschwitz, in the
> face of the unavenged murder of the whole Jewish people, in the
> light of the bestiality toward the elderly, women, and children, they
> continued to believe in God's special affection for the Jews. (p. 39)

Prisoners were not only known by their religious and ideological anchors. Reputations and fluid hierarchies were also based
on survival skills and professional reputations that preceded
Auschwitz. For some, such as Fania Fenelon, Szymon Laks,
Charlotte Delbo, and Jean Amery, identities as women and men
compete with other identities—musician, playwright, and philosopher—for "master status."

STATUS

Status or position within Auschwitz determined many survivor experiences and stories. Nowhere is this more evident than
in the words of Fenelon and Laks, two Auschwitz musicians. Once
he has survived the initial selection, Laks takes advantage of every
opportunity to improve his situation. He gives English lessons to
"two well-off Poles . . . They paid me with bread, margarine, and
potatoes" (p. 58). He eats well and is proud of his appearance: his
neatly cut hair and his custom-made striped suit. He describes this
suit in some detail: "The narrow-waisted jacket had a band on the
left pocket with the artistically drawn figures of my number and
the yellow and pink triangles making up the Star of David" (pp.
60–61).[5]

At one point he presents a picture of himself that is greatly
at odds with the images I have of Auschwitz prisoners, and tells
of his "considerable reserve of calories and health" (p. 109).

Laks' writing reflects status differences among Polish prisoners in their cultural status and musical skills. He writes in bewil-
derment at the lack of gratitude other Poles showed when he
attempted to correct their grammar:

> Someone called out, "Hey Felek, hand me that shoe laying
> there!" . . . I shouted out . . . "You say hand me that shoe lying
> there, not laying there." My brother musician, but not in race, got

down from the pallet, gave me two slaps, and screamed, "You, you lousy Jew, are you trying to teach a Pole to speak Polish?" (p. 104)

One of the primary sources of status among prisoners was the length of time they had been at Auschwitz. New prisoners are contemptuously called *zugangen*. As a new prisoner, Nomberg-Przytyk tells us:

> At Auschwitz the *zugangi* (new arrivals) were at the bottom of the ladder. They were pariahs who were treated contemptuously by the other prisoners. They were beaten and kicked mercilessly and endlessly. They constantly tormented themselves over the orders and commands that were unfamiliar to them and that they could not understand. *Zugangi*–the new prisoners who did not know how to "organize"–did not know how or where to hide; they made themselves absurd trying to defend their human dignity. Just for fun the *sztubowa* would beat a new prisoner in the face for a long time, until the eyes looked as if they were blue "eye-glasses." The new inmate would be so surprised that she would not even shield her face and would look around innocently and ask: "Why are you hitting me? I am a human being." The *sztubowa* would answer, "You are a *zugang*, a stinking *zugang*. For my part you can drop dead right now". . . .
>
> They [the more established and high status prisoners] spoke with such hatred and contempt to the *zugangen* as if the *zugangen* deserved nothing better than ill treatment and death. We existed only so they might have somebody to kick around, somebody to beat up on, somebody to serve as a background to their reflected glory. (pp. 19–20)

Laks writes with pride of his status as a long-term prisoner:

> My situation continued to improve, not only because of the position I had attained, but mainly because I had ceased to be scorned by all as a "millionaire." This was the name given by older prisoners with low numbers to newly arrived prisoners, who naturally got higher and higher numbers. We were now at number 130,000. And so my number, 49,543–a series from which very few were still alive–gave rise to universal respect. (p. 60)

Laks not only gives us a description of music at Auschwitz, but also clearly outlines the hierarchies of Nazi society in which Jewish prisoners were a subcategory of the lowest rank:

> The species generally called human had been divided into roughly four categories:

1. Supermen, or Aryan Germans who loved the Fuhrer and were obedient to his slogans and commands;

2. Men, or Aryan Germans who thought and acted differently than the Fuhrer ordered;

3. Submen, or all other Aryans; and finally

4. Vermin, or Jews, Gypsies, and other dregs of the two-legged community.

This division comes as no surprise, the surprise would be that it was accepted as gospel by the *prisoners themselves*. . . .

On the other hand, separate from this hierarchy and segregation practiced by everybody, there prevailed in the camp another, tacit ethic whose distinguishing mark was the date of arrival in Birkenau, indicated by the number tattooed on the left forearm and repeated on the band of the left jacket pocket: a low number meant a longer stay in the camp, survival of the first mental and physical shocks, fortitude, and aptitude for organizing; all of this gave rise to a certain respect not only from the "better" categories of *Haftlinge* but also from the esmen. (p. 102, 103)

Laks knows that his position in the orchestra is one of unparalleled privilege and luck, accounting for his survival for two and a half years where others did not live as many months.

. . . in every camp there were two separate categories of prisoners: the VIPs, who were well supplied, and the paupers, who were condemned to perpetual starvation, hard labor, illness, and death. (p. 118)

Laks is too honest to pretend that his music benefits these "paupers." He writes angrily of those who assert that music had any utility for the thousands of starving prisoners forced to march to the beat of his music as they go to and from the fields outside the camp: "I never *even once* met a prisoner whom music perked up and encouraged to survive. The motto of the starving was, eat, eat, eat . . ." (p. 118). Rather, he writes, "[m]usic kept up the 'spirit' (or rather the body) of only . . . the musicians, who did not have to go out to hard labor and could eat a little better" (p. 117).

Orchestra membership not only grants privileges. It also separates musicians from other prisoners, who define them as collaborators with the Germans, vultures who feed off the deaths of others. Fenelon tells us that as women march past the orchestra in the early morning, they yell out to the musicians, "Quitters, bitches, traitors!" (p. 46) Fenelon reacts with pain and tells us, "I [now] became aware of the farcical nature of this orchestra, conducted by this elegant woman, these comfortably dressed girls sitting on chairs playing to these virtual skeletons, shadows showing us faces which were faces no longer" (p. 46).

Other prisoners such as Delbo exclude women in the orchestra from the kinship of comradery. In their eyes, these musicians have their uniforms, their instruments, their very lives because less talented—or perhaps merely less fortunate—musicians have been murdered. Death contaminates everything:

> There are boarding-school girls wearing identical pleated skirts, their hats trailing blue ribbons . . . A band will be dressed in the girls' pleated skirts. The camp commandant wishes Viennese waltzes to be played every Sunday morning . . . Do not look at the violinist. She is playing on an instrument that could be Yehudi's if Yehudi were not miles away, on the other side of the ocean. Which Yehudi did this violin belong to? (pp. 6, 8, 107)

Other skills could also entitle a prisoner to certain jobs. Levi notes with irony that his degree in chemistry qualified him for particular work that was more physically demanding than many jobs without prerequisite examinations. Three months after his arrival at Auschwitz, Levi is told that he will take a chemistry examination to assess his qualifications for work as a chemist at Auschwitz:

> With these empty faces of ours, with these sheared craniums, with these shameful clothes, to take a chemical examination. And obviously it will be in German; and we will have to go in front of some blond Aryan doctor hoping that we do not have to blow our noses, because perhaps he will not know that we do not have handkerchiefs, and it will certainly not be possible to explain it to him. And we will have our old comrade hunger with us, and we will hardly be able to stand still on our feet, and he will certainly smell our odour, to which we are by now accustomed, but which persecuted us during the first days, the odour of turnips and cabbages, raw, cooked and digested. (1961, pp. 93–94)

Seven prisoners are to take the oral chemistry examination. Primo Levi is last. Alex, the Kapo of the Chemical Kommando, makes it clear that he judges Levi's chances for success as slim:

Alex looks at me blackly on the doorstep; he feels himself in some way responsible for my miserable appearance. He dislikes me because I am Italian, because I am Jewish and because, of all of us, I am the one furthest from his sergeants' mess ideal of virility. By analogy, without understanding anything, and proud of this very ignorance, he shows a profound disbelief in my chances for the examination.

We have entered. There is only Doktor Pannwitz; Alex, beret in hand, speaks to him in an undertone: ". . . an Italian, has been here only three months, already half kaputt . . . *Er sagt er is Chemiker* ('He says he is a chemist'). . ." (1959, pp. 95–96)

The examination begins.

I feel like Oedipus in front of the Sphinx. My ideas are clear, and I am aware even at this moment that the position at stake is important; yet I feel a mad desire to disappear, not to take the test. . . .

I took my degree in Turin in 1941, *summa cum laude*–and while I say it I have the definite sensation of not being believed, of not even believing it myself; it is enough to look at my dirty hands covered with sores, my convict's trousers encrusted with mud. Yet I am he, the B.Sc. of Turin, in fact, at this particular moment it is impossible to doubt my identity with him, as my reservoir of knowledge of organic chemistry, even after so long an inertia, responds at request with unexpected docility. And even more, this sense of lucid elation, this excitement which I feel warm in my veins, I recognize it, it is the fever of examinations, *my* fever of *my* examinations, that spontaneous mobilization of all my logical faculties and all my knowledge, which my friends at university so envied me. (1959, p. 97)

Levi and his friend Alberto pass the examination. Levi writes of the outcome, awarded months later:

We are the chemists, "therefore" we work at the phenylbeta sacks. . . . So far, the advantages of being in the Chemical Kommando have been limited to the following: the others carry 100 pound cement sacks, while we carry 125 pound phenylbeta sacks. How can we still think about the chemistry examination and our illusions of that time? (pp. 123–124)

Still, Levi looks to his profession for an organizing scheme. In *The Periodic Table* (1984), Levi uses the chemists' table of the elements as a metaphor for all of reality: Auschwitz, the Enlightenment, and the worlds of story and myth. He classifies his own family,

Piedmontese Jews, with their complex history of wandering, as "inert" elements. There is mystery and turmoil. But this chemist dreams of bringing rationality into a world of chaos.

REVERSALS

In re-reading the stories, I found not only patterns of location based on cultural differences, but also frequent examples of reversals of the gendered patterns identified by other readers and myself. Stories of chaos and death often overcame stories of resistance. I wondered, if women's patterns of survival were shaped by victimization, might not male voices from Auschwitz also reflect similar effects of victimization? And do not the voices of female and male survivors also reflect the brutality of Auschwitz that pitted each against all others? The first reading emphasized interpersonal relationships among women. In my second reading, I reframe valorization as a temptation to idealize women's stories and explore the powerlessness and reliance on interpersonal relationships in some male Auschwitz survivor stories, like Levi's. In such circumstances:

> . . . men's autobiographical practices might demonstrate patterns similar to women's . . . [such as] identity through group consciousness . . . It is no less true that what we have learned about autobiographical subjectivity from women's writing can produce new and suggestive readings of *canonical* male texts. (Miller 1994, p. 9)

For women as well as men, Auschwitz was not an ennobling experience. Friendships did not always triumph over betrayal. There were few opportunities for valor in this inferno. When I listen more closely to the men's voices, and not just to women's reports of men's behavior, I find many instances of community and mutual aid.

Laks writes at length of turning to music for solace in a world that he did not expect to leave alive. That he or anyone else survived is, for Laks, a miracle. In contrast to my earlier characterization of him as one who survives at any cost, he claims:

> I came out with my life. To what do I owe this? I did not have to get rid of a single ordinary human virtue, and yet I survived. For me there is no doubt that I owe this to an unending series of

miracles, but also, and perhaps above all, to my encounter with a few countrymen with a human face and a human heart. And there was frightfully little of this. (p. 19)

Years later, he answers one woman who asks with resentment why he survived when millions did not, "I'm sorry. . . . I didn't do it on purpose" (p. 15).

Laks discusses primarily the men of Auschwitz, and classifies them according to musical talent and appreciation. He easily forgives an SS who had recruited him to play cards, telling us that "[my] potential murderer became my savior" (p. 31). He further protects his "savior" by expressly not revealing his name to the reader and giving him a blessing. He refers to this SS officer as "my angel" (p. 33).

Let us return to the story of Lilith that was introduced in Chapter Three. On a second reading, its nine pages tell a complex tale of women and men and of the richness of storytelling. Levi simultaneously suggests and rejects that Lilith might be responsible for Auschwitz. Levi invites us to question stories, meanings, and even gender stereotypes. Levi's story of Lilith is a story situated within other stories, a story about stories, and of truths within conflicting truths. He tells us, "I won't guarantee that I myself didn't add something, and perhaps all who tell them add something: and that's how stories are born" (1979, p. 42). Levi does not guarantee the veracity of his story. Indeed, he deconstructs his story and confides to the Tischler, "[t]he stories [of Lilith] are many. I'll tell you a few of them, because it's our birthday and it's raining, and today my role is to tell and believe; you are the unbeliever today" (1979, p. 41). Levi seems to cross gender lines here by tasking some solace in storytelling—not a detached, intellectual type of storytelling, but emotionally involved and evocative.

Lilith has many guises: she is the first woman, the first to insist on "equal rights or nothing" (1979, p. 42), a she-devil, God's lover. Levi draws into question his version of the stories of Lilith, and we are left with this possibility for yet another story, her story.

Levi further complicates my attempts to classify his behavior according to gender stereotypes. He prefaces this story with the words of a woman physician who also survived Auschwitz, "How was I able to survive Auschwitz? My principle is: I come first, second, and third. Then nothing, then again I; and then all the others" (1988, p. 79).

When we look more closely at Fenelon's portrayal of Alma Rose, we find a character not unlike Laks. Like Laks, she arranges orchestra members' lives for the sake of musical quality. Rose explains to Fenelon:

> "I care about them all, though I prefer the good musicians, but that's natural. When they brought me Marta, a German born in Breslau, an excellent cellist although she was only seventeen, of course I was pleased. . . . I looked after her, I got her sister Renate put in Canada: one plays better when one's mind is at rest." (p. 121)

But all privileges have to be earned, and the women do not meet Rose's standards for musical quality. Rose refuses to ask Maria Mandel, commander of the women's camp, for extra food for the women because, "They spoilt my concert last Sunday; I'd be ashamed" (p. 103). Rose confides to Fenelon:

> "Frau Mandel asks me if the girls are hungry. Of course they're hungry, of course I could ask for food. But when they play so badly, is it not my duty to keep silent?" (p. 121)

Fenelon simultaneously places Alma Rose within a tradition of strong Jewish women and discounts her as inhuman. She quotes Rose, and judges her character:

> "I decided that strict discipline was the answer—they had dared claim to be musicians and they must prove it! I wouldn't let them massacre music!" Her dark eyes shone with the fanaticism of a Judith. Her passion made her beautiful and inhuman. (p. 120)

And as with Laks, the SS show this conductor a measure of respect and, perhaps, affection. Then Alma dies suddenly in 1944. The SS order an autopsy and diagnose poisoning. Maria Mandel tells the women of the orchestra, "Your conductor, Alma Rose, is dead. You may go to the Revier and pay her your last respects." The women file past the casket:

> In a sort of recess to the medical room the SS had put up a catafalque covered with white flowers—a profusion, an avalanche of flowers, mainly lilies, and giving off an amazingly strong scent. . . . we all began to cry. Some SS came in, removed their hats, and

filed past the foot of her bed. All were visibly moved and many
were crying. . . . Here, tears in their eyes, the SS bowed down
before the corpse of a Jewess they'd covered with white flowers.
(p. 208)

What can be taken for callousness in stories of male survivors can
also be merely the result of being too overwhelmed by exhaustion
and ubiquitous death to recognize the humanity of other prisoners. "I recall," Amery writes, "times when I climbed heedlessly
over piled-up corpses and all of us were too weak or indifferent
even to drag the dead out of the barracks into the open" (p. 15).
Early on, Amery has not yet developed the ability to *not* feel, an
ability necessary for survival:

> I had not yet adjusted to the terror in the camp. The suffering
> and dying of those others whom I ran into at every step still did
> not just roll off my back. I had not yet cast off the thin skin of the
> *zugang*. This came later. Unless you sloughed off that skin you could
> not survive in Auschwitz. (p. 39)

In spite of his disclaimers for emotionality, Amery places an
extremely high value on being loved. In his soul-searching chapter on "The Necessity and Impossibility of Being a Jew," he
explicitly equates being loved with being human. All of Germany,
he writes, "denied that we [Jews] were worthy of being loved and
thereby worthy of life" (p. 87). And as I re-read Amery's story of
his bunkmate, I am struck with differences among the men. Home
for one means meals with loved ones. For another it is the intellectual life of books and language. For others home means work,
colleagues, family and ethnic heritage, city life, or the country-
side. Men as well as women at Auschwitz forged traces of home
life: through friendships, sharing food, literature, or music, and
dreams of returning. Each remains alone with his memories and
his losses.

It is not difficult to find support for reversals of the stereotypi-
cal gender roles in these stories. Each story contains instances in
which women and men violated gendered norms for behavior
and reasoning. Males, too, write of turning to each other for
personal support—support that goes far beyond material aid or instrumental rationality. Bereft of kin, Levi forms deep and intimate

friendships with other men. In *Survival in Auschwitz,* he remembers his friend Alberto:

> I did not manage to gain permission to sleep in a bunk with him. . . . It is a pity . . . it is winter now and the nights are long, and since we are forced to exchange sweats, smells and warmth with someone under the same blanket, and in a width little more than two feet, it is quite desirable that he be a friend. (1959, pp. 51–52)

This could not be taken for granted, for, as Laks writes:

> Hostility between neighbors of the same pallet was dreadfully human and understandable. One got in the way of another; each one took up more space than he supposedly should have. I curled up as much as I could, which enabled me to gain the good graces of my neighbors, and somehow settled down to longed-for sleep. (p. 22–23)

Levi credits his survival to Lorenzo, not so much for his "material aid," but by his "goodness." For Lorenzo showed Levi "that there still existed a just world outside our own, something and someone still pure and whole, not corrupt, not savage, extraneous to hatred and terror; something difficult to define, a remote possibility of good, but for which it was worth surviving" (1959, p. 111).

I also found Laks breaking away from conventional male patterns of behavior and language. He writes of loneliness, and of friendships with intrinsic value: "Sudden fear came over me on account of my loneliness" (p. 35). He and Ludwich Zuk-Skarszewski, a friend from Auschwitz, each assumed the other was dead. Thirty years later Laks meets Aleksander Kulisiewicz, a former prisoner of Sachenhausen and a collector of concentration camp music and poetry, and learns that Zuk is alive and teaching near Krakow: "It took Aleksander Kulisiewicz's collecting bug to rekindle a friendship that had been buried so long ago. What words should be used to celebrate such rediscoveries? I will not use any. Since that time we have been writing to each other regularly" (p. 13–14). While he speaks glowingly of Germans in their love of music, it is three men, all Polish Jews, of whom he writes with great warmth. In fact, it is their humanity, not their material assistance, that he remembers with gratitude. They are "stars that will shine for me until my dying day. . . . who spoke to me as one equal to another, as one man to another, Pole to Pole, Jew to Jew. . . . Thanks to them I felt like a human being again" (pp. 104–105). As with Fenelon, Laks tells the stories of his friends in detail. He has corresponded with them long beyond liberation.

Neither are male survivors' stories always coherent and closed. In Amery's preface to the 1977 edition of his book (first published in 1966) he writes:

> I had no clarity when I was writing this little book, I do not have it today, and I hope that I never will. Clarification would also amount to disposal, settlement of the case, which can then be placed in the files of history. My book is meant to aid in preventing precisely this. (p. xxi)

There are not only tales of sisterhood among women prisoners, there are also accounts of jealousy and squabbling. Nomberg-Przytyk recounts frequent and violent fights:

> over a place in the food line, over a drink of water, over a potato in the soup. . . . there would be fights over bread that women stole from under each other's pillows. They cried in desperation, yelled, and pounced at each other's eyes. (p. 4)

Even the sworn friendship between Fania Fenelon and Clara is short-lived. Fenelon speaks repeatedly of the conflicts that develop between Clara and the other women of the orchestra. Clara betrays them all as she trades in their friendship for affiliation with the powerful of Auschwitz. Clara is now a Kapo:

> Clara rose up before us, arm band in place, club in hand . . . now she had lost even such humanity as had remained to her. Everything that was left of the timid, bashful young girl had just disappeared, destroyed once and for all by the environment of the camp. (p. 243)

Fania tries in vain to appeal to the Clara she had known months before:

> "Clara, look at yourself! You've become a monster. If you lash out at our friends, you'll never dare to go back home. Remember your childhood, your girlhood, your parents . . . Clara look at yourself!"

> Her eyes shone with a positively mineral brightness, like coals. "Be quiet and listen to me. I'm through with your superior airs, your moralizing. Here, it's me who's the stronger, it's me who's in charge. I've heard enough, now get away!" (p. 244)

Nomberg-Przytyk also describes the "chain of cruelty" that placed newcomers at the bottom. Those with positions of relative privilege used whatever methods were necessary to assure their own survival and their relatively comfortable way of life: "Cruelty towards the weak and humility towards the strong was the rule here" (pp. 20–21).

In carefully re-reading these stories, I had to relinquish images of universal female superiority in Auschwitz. I've learned that not only is there no one "true story" of Auschwitz, neither is there any one true pattern to its stories.[6] Individual and collective stories form complementary and overlapping access to truths of the past. I am reminded by Lowenthal in his writings on memory and history that "the truth in history is not the only truth about the past; every story is true in countless ways" (1985, p. 229).

The dehumanization of Auschwitz demands that I honor individual stories and move away from the belief that I could ever think about lived experiences of the event without attending to its many stories. Comfortable and comprehensible as myths of unfailing heroism may be, the accompanying risk of totalitarianism outweighs its appeal. As Arendt powerfully argues, fascism and all forms of totalitarianism depend on the consistency of one sanctioned truth, "the story" (1973, p. 352). Lyotard's writings echo Arendt's observations. Plurality is "one of the basic existential conditions of human life" (Lyotard 1978, p. 74). People who insist that some remnant of the individual's story can be salvaged rebel against a fascist ideology of anonymity and total domination. They defamiliarize monolithic and dichotomous conceptions of that time and place, making what once seemed familiar now seem strange.

The ultimate reality of Auschwitz, however, determined that prisoner status superseded all other identities and categories. Listening carefully to Auschwitz stories, I cannot stop my ears to the chaos in and between survivors' words.

NOTES

1. It would be most interesting, but beyond the scope of this work, to address questions of why cultural feminism has been appealing—for others, but also at times for me.

2. In 1992 Sidonie Smith and Julia Watson edited a collection of essays on gender and women's autobiography. They aptly note that "locations in gender, class, race, ethnicity, and sexuality complicate one another . . . . Neither can one be oblivious to the precise location in which the subject is situated" (pp. xiv–xv). Autobiography must be placed within its sociohistorical context.

3. This incident was also etched permanently in Daniele's mind. When the two met again, months later in Byelorussia, Daniele accused Levi, "Why the two of you and not I?" (1988, pp. 80–81)

4. The "room elders," "room overseers" or "room leaders," assistants to the *blokowa*, whose job was to maintain order among prisoners (Nomberg-Przytyk p. 184).

5. At Auschwitz the pink triangle indicated an inmate's status as a homosexual. Jews were usually identified by a Star of David—a red triangle sewn over a yellow triangle (Czech 1990, p. 364). Except for comments on the attractiveness of young male prisoners, this is Laks' only reference in his memoir to his sexual preference.

6. See also Young for explorations of interrelationships between pasts of the Holocaust and evolving contexts in the present. His earlier work (1988) centers on literary texts, while his more recent (1991, 1993) examine Holocaust memorials as texts of collected memory.

CHAPTER 5

Chaos

Pack in all my blackened pots,
Their split lids, the chipped crockeries,
Pack in my chaos with its gold-encrusted buttons
Since chaos will always be in fashion.

–Kadia Molodowsky 1976

The need to honor chaos stories is both moral and
clinical. . . . To deny a chaos story is to deny the
person telling this story. . . . The challenge is to
hear. . . .

–A. W. Frank 1995, p. 109

Journal Entry: December 10, 1994

It is cold, dry and windy. I am visiting my brother, Rob, in Chicago for the weekend. We have spent the morning at the Museum of Science and Industry, and my young niece and nephew need naps. Felix Nussbaum's "Carnival Group" is on display at the Smart Museum of Art at the University of Chicago nearby, and I talk Rob into stopping there with me on our way back to his house. Parking is free and close by. Mary, Rob's wife, stays with the napping children in the car while we run in.

I have been interested in this painting for several months. I first noticed it on the cover of the January 27, 1993, issue of *JAMA*, the *Journal of the American Medical Association*, that I occasionally peruse when preparing lectures for classes in medical sociology. I have made it a habit to read the short articles on the art work found on each issue's cover. This time I take additional notice. The artist, Felix Nussbaum, lived in Europe from 1904–1944. A Jew, he moved from Germany to Belgium in 1935. The Nazis arrested

Nussbaum in 1940 and sent him to St. Cyprien, a French internment camp. From there he escaped four months later, and returned to Belgium. He spent the next four years in hiding, painting. He completed "Carnival" in 1939. On July 31, 1944, Nussbaum was captured and deported to Auschwitz. He died there in the gas chambers on August 3, 1944. His works were forgotten, stored in basements and attics of friends and relatives for almost thirty years. In 1970, art critic Wendelin Zimmer first heard of Nussbaum's paintings, and began a long process of rediscovering and publicizing Nussbaum's works.

The Smart Museum of Art opened in 1974. Already its single floor is crowded with displays. The information desk attendant has never heard of the painting and is busy helping set up chairs and music stands for a concert in the lobby later that day. Knowing that the painting was completed around 1939, we head for the rear of the building and Room 8, "Mid-20th Century." On the far wall, partially blocked by a lucite stand containing miniature sculptures, we find the "Carnival Group."

The colors are deeper and warmer than any reproduction of the painting I have seen. The frame is plain dark brown, setting off the picture without detracting from the stark wasteland depicted. The figures' eyes stare over my left shoulder, follow me, but never meet mine.

Nussbaum groups multiple carnivalistic self-portraits as female, male, and androgenous. Against a backdrop of rural and urban devastation, Nussbaum stares out beyond us as a woman in an artist's cap, her right hand covering her mouth. As a woman in a triangular medieval hat, Nussbaum screams out of a twisted mouth and squinting, empty black eyes. There is a wide-eyed man in a black top hat peering over the heads of the others. Their hats *conceal his mouth. Rob finds him frightening. The man is simultaneously absent and omnipresent, sorrowful and depraved. The museum catalogue says the top hat means this is a German burgher. But in a skull cap and prayer shawl, his mouth obliterated by a blur of brush strokes, Nussbaum is also a silenced orthodox Jewish man. His juxtaposed images of himself challenge our categorizations: gender and nationality, vision and voice, carnival and devastation.*

Like Nussbaum's self portraits, the representations Auschwitz survivors offer of themselves and others are too messy to be encased in categories of thought—whether of gender, nationality, or occupation. Each category dissolves into fragmentation and chaos. Every supposed pattern is subject to rupture by counter-example and stories on altogether divergent planes. Auschwitz has, in the words of survivors, systematically demolished pre-existing ways in which individuals understand and situate themselves within the world. Survivors write of Auschwitz not as a microcosm of the known world but as a world of chaos in which the norms by which they have ordered their lives have been annihilated. Delbo tells us, "one couldn't be sustained by one's past, draw on its resources. It had become unreal, unbelievable. Everything that had been our previous existence had unraveled" (p. 168). In a similar vein, Fenelon writes, "death, life, tears, laughter, everything was multiplied, disproportionate, beyond the limits of the credible. All was madness" (p. 70).

Many survivors describe an abyss between themselves and their captors. For Levi, prisoners and captors not only belong to different worlds; they are different beings (1959, p. 96). The prisoners have been stripped of their names, but the Nazis have retained both their titles and their names. A "Doctor Pannwitz" interrogates Levi as "Haftling 174517" in a life or death oral chemistry examination.[1] Levi writes:

> Pannwitz is tall, thin, blond; he has eyes, hair, and nose as all Germans ought to have them, and sits formidably behind a com-

plicated writing-table. I, Haftling 174517, stand in his office, which is a real office, shining, clean and ordered, and I feel that I would leave a dirty stain on whatever I touched. (1959, p. 96)

Their eyes meet, but "that look was not one between two men; . . . [but] between two beings who live in different worlds" (1959, p. 96). Levi does well on the brief examination. He recalls, "my reservoir of knowledge of organic chemistry . . . responds at request with unexpected docility. . . . It is as if I was trying to remember the events of a previous incarnation" (1959, p. 97). Levi is pleased with his performance, but unsure of the verdict. He leaves awkwardly:

> I know how to say to eat, to work, to steal, to die in German; I also know how to say sulfuric acid, atmospheric pressure, and short-wave generator, but I do not know how to address a person of importance. . . . What is certain is that I have spent a day without working, so that tonight I will have a little less hunger, and this is a concrete advantage, not to be taken away. (1959, pp. 97–98)

Especially for survivors from the bottom of Auschwitz's hierarchy, attempts to locate themselves in the chaos of Auschwitz falter and spill over into worlds beyond. Delbo writes of stopping in Berlin with a group of French women prisoners, guarded by the SS and on their way to Ravensbruck in January, 1944:

> Suddenly we heard someone shouting in French, "This way, pal!" We called out at once, "Hey, hey, over there! Hey, Frenchmen! You're French? We're Frenchwomen!" A man turns around, gives us an unpleasant look, muttering, "Merde!" then takes off at a run to jump into a train across from our track.
> "For the first Frenchman we see . . . what a greeting!" says Lulu.
> We were deeply disappointed. How is it possible! Women wearing striped uniforms call out, and this free man does not even ask who they are, where they're coming from. We came from Auschwitz. Everyone should have realized it. We discovered an abyss between the world and us, and it made us very sad. (p. 181)

In this reading, individual stories join together, not in narrative wholes, but in jarring fragments. Gendered dichotomies have splintered into situated utterances that complement and enrich each other, and are in turn drowned out by discordant cacophony.

THE GROTESQUE

Gold, in Yiddish poet Kadia Molodowsky's words, is no longer an emblem of beauty, purity, and abundance.[2] It evokes images of golden teeth torn from corpses' mouths, of tarnish and decay. In the stories of Auschwitz, attempts by prisoners to maintain or create situated identities often give way to overwhelming and grotesque debasement. The grotesque, according to Mikhail Bakhtin (1984, pp. 19–20), has at its core total inversion and degradation. The grotesque world of Auschwitz is an ugly upside-down world, a world of the bizarre, the incongruous, and the irrational. "Grotesque" reflects the horror of games of life and death played out under conditions of hierarchical and absolute power over life and death. "Grotesque" reflects feeble efforts of those without power to subvert the bizarre totality in which they are immersed, where prisoners know their "tormenters were toying with us" (Nomberg-Przytyk, p. 12).

Survivors' use of humor–at first glance entirely out of place in an Auschwitz story–is best understood as a grotesque form of resistance within parameters set by the SS. On arrival at Auschwitz, and after selection at the ramp, Fenelon temporarily reflects, "'I wouldn't actually come here for a Christmas holiday, of course,' I said jokingly. 'The staff haven't quite been licked into shape yet; they're not what you'd call considerate'" (p. 17).

Later, under infinitely more oppressive circumstances, resistance takes the form of subtle subversion of rules against playing Jewish music. Fenelon disguises works of Jewish composers so that "the women in the work groups marched off to the rhythm of Jewish music, and some of them clearly recognized it. Not a single SS ever noticed" (p. 125). She includes a piece by Mendelssohn on a program for the SS and titles it "Violin Concerto." She is confident that "None of them is bright enough to notice" (p. 125). Even German music can be subversive in Fenelon's hands:

> Alma had wanted some Beethoven; I claimed that all I could remember was the first movement of the Fifth Symphony and I suggested she put it on the programme. A rare pleasure for me. She didn't see any malice in it, nor did the SS. They saw no connection with the signature tune of the Free French broadcasts

on the BBC. For them it was Beethoven, a god, a monument to German music, and they listened to it in respectful rapture. Their lack of a sense of humour was almost touching. There was intense jubilation when our orchestra played the piece. It was one of my most perfect moments. (p. 106)

Fenelon summarizes her use of carnivalistic humor at Auschwitz: "It was amusing to be able to sing a song of hope under their noses. Guile is the revenge of the weak" (p. 125).

Delbo too, speaks of laughter—a silent mocking laughter, the "ambivalent . . . deriding . . . laughter of carnival" (Bakhtin 1984, p. 12) that turns suffering into a surrealistic horror. She tells of running a gauntlet of blows from clubs and belts, and compares herself to a disembodied and decapitated duck. "And then I felt like laughing. Or rather, I saw my double who wanted to laugh" (p. 38).

Auschwitz humor is short-lived, ultimately an oxymoron. Shortly before liberation, Fenelon and the other Jewish members of the orchestra were transferred to Bergen-Belsen, where conditions were much harder. There is little humor in this section of Fenelon's story, and what is there is desperate and lonely. Only from a distance of thirty years can Fenelon reflect on her condition after five months at Bergen-Belsen with anything approaching irony. She writes, "The bones must have broken through the skin. Or had the hand actually come off? Impossible. I must keep my hands to play the piano. Play the piano . . . those knucklebones at the end of my arm might just manage *Danse Macabre*. The idea actually made me laugh" (p. 3).

The grotesque can lend a form of resistance to oppression. In fact, by the sheer fact of survival, any Auschwitz survivor is a resisting subject. But when applied to Auschwitz, Bakhtin's use of the "grotesque" can be problematic. It would be most inappropriate and inaccurate to suppose that the grotesque character of Auschwitz contains emancipatory potential in itself. Bakhtin allows for potential emancipation in the grotesque, and minimizes the effect of power.

In Bakhtin's description of carnival, power relationships are also inverted and subverted, albeit only temporarily, and with the tacit approval of those in power. I became increasingly uncomfortable with the notion of carnival as applied to Auschwitz. It presumes too much autonomy on the part of inmates, and eventual return to pre-existing social order. There is an emancipatory moment in carnival, a hint of the temporality of power relationships, that does not hold with the truths of Auschwitz. To simply call Auschwitz a "carnival" makes a mockery of unimaginable suffering.[3]

In spite of its game-like qualities for a privileged few (games of deception, subversion, and power), Auschwitz was anything but play. The first-person stories we have are from those who, through timing, privilege, powerful connections, and luck, survived. It is easy to read valor and purposeful subversion and agency into their stories, and to project these characteristics onto all who disembarked from the trains at Auschwitz. But we know better. The grotesque of Auschwitz is cruel and ugly, with little redemption.

Each work speaks of dehumanization of victims. It includes what Levi calls "useless violence" as well as degradation with evident intent. Survivors describe chaos and degradation on arrival at Auschwitz: from loss of all personal possessions to the humiliation of public nakedness and shaving, from separation from family members and friends to forfeiting names for numbers, from treatment unimaginable for cattle to the Babel of camp languages. Prisoners' clothes were typically impractical and outrageous. Shortly after arrival at Auschwitz, Nomberg-Przytyk and those who arrived with her were given new clothes: "In the next room we were given any old rags that were handy. I was given a long, black, silk dress, full of holes, and nothing beside that. Outside there was a very hard frost. For our feet they gave us wooden clogs and no stockings" (p. 15). Survivors also describe meaningless, life-draining work, total lack of privacy, betrayal, living in excrement. Even death was bereft of any notice or dignity. Fenelon recounts "one of the aims of National Socialism: the destruction of human dignity" (p. 133).

Amery brilliantly captures the bureaucratic violence that characterized Nazi operations. He describes his torture by the SS: "The boundaries of my body are also the boundaries of myself.

My skin surface shields me against the external world. If I am to have trust, I must feel on it only what I *want* to feel" (p. 30). "Whoever was tortured, stays tortured. Torture is erratically burned into him, even when no clinically objective traces can be detected" (p. 34).

Torture was not some "accidental quality." It was "the essence" of Auschwitz. Perhaps we should understand the existential–yet permanent and definitive–effects of absolute power. In speaking of torture, Amery appropriates the language of sexual violation, and comes close to capturing Fenelon's brutal sexual imagery. He writes, "I dare to assert that torture is the most horrible event a human being can retain within himself. . . . It is like a rape, a sexual act without the consent of one of the two partners" (pp. 22, 28). It is a permanent violation of one's very core of being. Amery unashamedly condemned all attempts to find meaning in or through the Holocaust and his experiences of torture and imprisonment.

In the writings of women from Auschwitz, beauty turns grotesque, betrays, and is not to be trusted. Fenelon tells us that Cyla, a *blokowa*, one of the elite prisoners, is beautifully dressed, and "looked like an angel. But every prisoner feared her" (p. 33). She writes repeatedly of the beauty of the cruelest SS officers, in particular Lagerfuhrerin Maria Mandel:

> This was the first time a representative of the German race had looked at me, had seemed to be aware of my presence. She took off her cap and her hair was a wonderful golden blond, done in thick plaits round her head. . . . I noted everything about her: her face, without a trace of makeup (forbidden by the SS) was luminous, her white teeth large but fine. She was perfect, too perfect. A splendid example of the master race: top-quality breeding material–so what was she doing here instead of reproducing? (p. 30)

Fenelon's description of Mandel left me with a picture of icy perfection; cruel and yet safely remote. But there is more. Toward the end of her story about Mandel, Fenelon presents a scene that chilled me more than any analysis ever could. Mandel adopts a beautiful Polish baby whose mother has just been gassed, and dresses him in "the most expensive clothes, a little blue sailor suit, and he looked adorable" (p. 226). For days, Mandel petted the child and took him with her throughout the camp. Fenelon sets the stage for the shock of betrayal, describing Mandel's show of affection for the child: "Seated on a chair in our music room, the child on her knee, she was delighted when we clustered round her, as proud as a mother" (p. 226). But in the end, "Mandel herself had taken the child to the gas chamber" (p. 227).

Nowhere was beauty so deliberately used for betrayal as by Dr. Mengele, the most infamous Nazi physician at Auschwitz. Fenelon describes his visit to listen to the women's orchestra:

> After a perfectly calculated pause the head surgeon made his entry. He was handsome. Goodness, he was handsome. So handsome the girls instinctively rediscovered the forgotten motions of another world, running dampened fingers through their lashes to make them shine, biting their lips, swelling their mouths, pulling at their skirts and tops. Under the gaze of this man one felt oneself become a woman again. . . . Dr. Mengele wore his uniform with incomparable ease and style. . . A smile played over his lips. Insouciantly he laughed and joked, conscious of his charm. (p. 159)

The handsome charm of this physician was commingled with death. Nomberg-Przytyk describes Mengele as, "that monster in the body of an Adonis" (p. 55) in the infirmary and on the selection ramp:

> Mengele gave us the most trouble. He was so handsome that he inspired trust. He would make himself comfortable in a chair and then become engrossed in conversation. The newly arrived women would forget where they were and start describing all their ailments. . . . These women did not realize that they were signing their own death warrants. . . .
>
> At the very entrance to the bath house stood the camp doctor, the celebrated Mengele, beautiful, elegant, with a smile that inspired trust. With a careless motion of his hand he directed some to the right and some to the left. Women with children, old people, the weak and the sick were on one side of the ramp. The young and healthy were on the other side. In front of Mengele everything was silent. There was no conversation. Everybody went in the direction casually indicated by the stick, not knowing that a verdict of life or death had just been pronounced on them. No one with a normal mind could comprehend this Hell. (pp. 56, 58–59)

In the words of Auschwitz survivors, the world of Auschwitz is not only without precedence, but also totally alien, totally other.[4]

It is another planet, an upside-down world, a betrayal of all expectations, a surrealistic nightmare.[5] Auschwitz survivor David Rousset writes in his memoir, *The Other Kingdom*, "Normal men don't know that everything is possible. Even if the evidence forces their intelligence to admit it, their muscles do not believe it" (1947, p. 168). Hannah Arendt (1973) reflected on Rousset's words and concluded that the total domination and unreality of Auschwitz remains the essence of Nazi totalitarianism. The central goal and purpose of Auschwitz was, Arendt concluded "total domination." The machinery of Auschwitz went beyond the nihilistic principle that "everything is permitted" (Arendt 1973, p. 440) and demonstrated that in this world, "everything is possible" (Aaron 1993).[6] Survivor stories of Auschwitz as an alien world challenge any notions I might have that the world is manageably safe. All that is familiar and gives order to life also has the power to betray. Culture and language can take on new and twisted meanings. Good and evil, time and rationality, language and culture: the contours can become unrecognizable.

GOOD AND EVIL

One of the most difficult and unanswerable questions raised by the Holocaust is the question of theodicy, of suffering that is unconnected to good or evil, that challenges notions of a just god. In these survivor stories, there is little overt reference to questions of theodicy. These survivors have perhaps left those questions to philosophers and theologians. What is more immediate in their stories is the obliteration of moral frameworks that define, reward, and punish good and evil.

Nomberg-Przytyk's subtitle tells us that her book is a collection of "true tales from a grotesque land." Within layer after layer of story, Nomberg-Przytyk insists that the reader question simple dichotomies of good and evil, of innocent and guilty. Of one prisoner, a German communist, she writes, "I had heard many different stories about her . . . in each situation she was a different person . . . I cannot judge Orli. I will not even try" (p. 41). And of another, a religious Slovakian, she writes, "[They] told me stories about Cyla . . . When she first came to the camp, she was barely fifteen years old . . . She came from a well-to-do Jewish family, religious and highly respected" (pp. 53, 54). "Today," Nomberg-Przytyk concludes, "she is eighteen years old and has the heart of a criminal capable of committing murder" (p. 55). Perhaps, Nomberg-Przytyk suggests, any of us could be Cyla.

Familiar scenes are ripe with betrayal: a drink of water, a flower, young children at play—each is twisted beyond recognition. In Delbo's tale, two healthy little boys play outside their home—but they are playing an ugly game of commandant and prisoner (pp. 98–100). It is the grotesque taken to the extreme, in which "all that was familiar for us and friendly suddenly becomes hostile" (Bakhtin 1984, p. 48).

Another example of betrayal, found in a short chapter by Delbo titled "The Tulip," concerns a pink tulip in the window of a house that Delbo and the other women prisoners pass on their way to work. The house itself speaks of home: "The chimney is smoking. . . . We can see white curtains. Muslin curtains. We utter 'Muslin' softly in the mouth. And in front of the curtains, in the space between the window and the storm sash, there is a tulip" (p. 60). The flower is "pink between two pale leaves . . . [a] pink beaker between pale leaves" (p. 61). The house brings reminiscence of a world beyond the camp, and dreams for a return to that world. They dream of this single flower and at roll call whisper to each other, "We saw a tulip" (p. 61). A few days later, the women learn that the house belongs to an SS officer of the camp. They feel bitterly betrayed: "[w]e despised this memory and the tender feeling which had not yet dried up within us" (p. 61). Harsh realities of camp existence shatter their images of a home radiating with beauty, safety, and warmth.

Betrayal encompasses the lives and deaths of children and holiday celebrations. In *Useless Knowledge,* Delbo titles a chapter "The Teddy Bear." This is a story of a Christmas meal, complete with beans, cabbage, potatoes with onion sauce and poppy seeds, beer, cigarettes, candles, a tree, and gifts. The women don silk stockings, white collars, even flowers for their hair. They have spent days "organizing" (camp jargon for a complex process of bribery and/or stealing) these items, and now open their gifts with joy:

"a cake of soap, a rag doll, a hand-made bow, a woven rope belt, a colorfully bound memorandum book" (p. 166), and finally:

> . . . a teddy bear! A small child's teddy. . . . This is how a doll, a teddy bear, arrives in Auschwitz. In the arms of a little girl who will leave her toy with her clothing, carefully folded, at the entrance to "the showers." A prisoner from the "heaven commando," as they called those who worked in the crematoria, had found it among the objects piled up in the showers' antechamber and exchanged it for a couple of onions. (p. 166)

More than any other Auschwitz story, this one has haunted me against my will. For each of my sons, now eleven and fifteen years old, I made a teddy bear for his first Christmas. Today the bears are well loved and threadbare. They no longer accompany us on every trip, but they are waiting for us when we return. Even in my imagination I cannot take myself through the necessary steps leading to the narrative point where Benji and Benny, the bears I sewed, could be organized as Christmas gifts, paid for by a couple of Auschwitz onions—and two more gassings.

Images of mothers, so comforting in other passages, become images of terror. Delbo dreams of returning home:

> [A]ll your relatives you assumed tormented by your absence turn their backs on you, grown mute and strange in their indifference. You say again: "It's me, I'm here . . . This time it's real, it's true since I'm in the kitchen, I'm touching the sink. You see, mama, it's me," but the cold of the stone sink propels me out of my dream. (p. 56)

In Auschwitz, prisoners did not so much transcend categories that shape our social worlds, as find all categories grotesquely twisted by an impossible logic of dehumanization and the almost futile possibility of survival. Delbo despairingly contrasts the sterilization of the women and the men, and concludes: "What difference does it make since none of them will return, since none of us will return" (p. 96).

In Auschwitz, I read: "women and children [come] first, they are the most exhausted" (Delbo 1995, p. 4), but for death, not life.[7] Nomberg-Przytyk writes, "Here in Auschwitz the German thugs murdered women and children first" (p. 80). In such a place what can it mean to be a parent? Nomberg-Przytyk tells of attempts women made to save their children or themselves:

> Imagine. I unpack a valise, and find a dead girl in it. She must have been about two years old. The mothers hid the children in the hope that once they got them into the camp they and the children would remain together. (p. 76)

Just twenty pages later, Nomberg-Przytyk has told the same story—with one important difference. In this telling, she contends that en route to Auschwitz some mothers hid their infants in suitcases in attempts to save themselves at the cost of their children (p. 98). Arriving at Auschwitz, a woman alone had hope of being judged fit for work. Mothers and their young children could expect to be sent to the gas chambers. "Here," Delbo tells us, "mothers are no longer mothers to their children" (p. 12).

In survivor stories the lines between good and evil are blurred and "meanings passed beyond the accepted boundaries of conventional significance" (Nomberg-Przytyk, p. 72).[8] It is a place where, in Amery's words, "there are no natural rights, and moral categories come and go like the fashions" (p. 11).

TIME, PLACE, AND RATIONALITY

In this reading, grotesque violence emerges as the essence of Auschwitz's institutional organization. Many survivors write of their post-Auschwitz existence as a wrenching split between their day-to-day lives and their memories of horror. It is eternally present.

Delbo's words, even after liberation, are permeated by a disembodied unreality. She has split from herself, and "[A]ll gestures had abolished themselves. . . . Our bodies walked outside us" (p. 35). She can no longer rely upon her senses to locate herself. Delbo writes, "I can't recall my own smell when I lifted my dress. Which proves that our nostrils were besmirched with our own stink and could no longer smell anything" (p. 150). At times Delbo tells her story as a nightmarish surrealistic theater. She weaves together past and present, then and now, here and there in an eternal present. All takes place in a "place where time is abolished. . . . time outside of time" (p. 32), where "[i]t is day for a whole eternity" (p. 48). Auschwitz is "a station that has no name" (p. 5), "a nameless town" (p. 14), "a nameless place" (p. 137), "a place before geography" (p. 167). She names her chapters: "Daytime," "One Day," "The Next Day," and "The Same Day;" time beyond time. Even the present is oddly one with the past: "I am writing this story in a cafe—it is turning into a story. A break in the clouds. Is it afternoon? We have lost all notion of time" (pp. 26–27).

Levi's words are similar. He writes, "Today, at this very moment as I sit writing at a table, I myself am not convinced that these things really happened" (1959, p. 94). The abyss between past and present, between memory and the writing of memories, is too immense to comprehend.

Auschwitz is a world where, Delbo writes, "one struggles against all reason" (p. 15) and where words are no longer capable of "recalling reason" (p. 70). There is, to use Horkheimer's phrase, "an eclipse of reason" (1974). Those arriving at Auschwitz "expect the worst—not the unthinkable" (Delbo, p. 4). It is a world where knowledge leads to death: "it would have been far better never to have entered, never to have found out" (Delbo, p. 9). The refrain of "Just try and see" (pp. 84, 85) turns to a cry of "Do not look. Do not listen" (p. 107). Those who know "were howling because they knew, but their vocal cords had snapped in their throats" (p. 34). Delbo concludes the second book of her Auschwitz trilogy, *Useless Knowledge*, with these words to the reader:

> *I know myself through and through/ a knowledge/ born from the depths of despair/ You find out soon enough/ you should not speak with death/ for it is a useless knowledge. . . . I have returned from a world beyond knowledge/ and now must unlearn/ for otherwise I clearly see/ that I can no longer live/ After all/ better not to believe/ these ghostly tales/ for if you do/ you'll never sleep again/ if you believe/ these ghostly phantoms/ revenants returning/ yet unable to tell/ how. (pp. 225, 230–231)*

One of the most ironic features of Auschwitz was the juxtaposition of order and chaos, military-like precision and filth, culture and barbarism, orchestras and torture. For Levi, rational behavior—the very idea of rationality, at Auschwitz—is inherently ironic.

In a chapter entitled "Useless Violence," Levi describes the degrading and militaristic "bed-making" ritual. In his telling, the scene resembles a grotesque episode from the "Key-Stone Cops"—but the objective is survival, not comedy.[9] The "beds" were wood planks, mattresses were thin and filled with wood shavings; pillows were torn and filled with straw; two men slept in each bed. After reveille, all beds had to be made "immediately," "simultaneously," and "perfectly." "It was therefore necessary for the occupants of the lower bunks to manage as best they could to fix mattress and blanket between the legs of the tenants of the upper levels" (1988, p. 117).

Levi describes the "frantic moments" during *bettenbaum*: "The atmosphere filled with dust to the point of becoming opaque, with . . . curses exchanged in all languages." After this frenzy of activity, "each bed must look like a rectangular parallelepiped with well-smoothed edges, on which was placed the smaller parallelepiped of the pillow." There were, of course, consequences. Anyone who did not properly make the bed was "punished publicly and savagely" (1988, p. 117).[10]

Laks also writes of absurd military-style rituals, including bed-making:

> My greatest nightmare was the bedspreads, or rather blankets, we had been issued and which, after reveille, had to be folded in a special, impeccable way, strictly according to the regulations. These light-brown blankets with the ghastly emblem of the Waffen SS were notorious for the obstinacy and recalcitrance, which could be overcome only with the greatest difficulty. And when an inspection by the *Blockfuhrer* was announced, more than one musician preferred to sleep on the floor rather than disturb the perfect folds of the blankets so arduously arranged the day before. (p. 43)

For Laks the ritual of saluting is even more absurd:

> the collective, ceremonial, synchronized (ideally) saluting at the command of our fellow prisoner-executioners. This was a real art, and more than one paid with his life for the inability to learn it.
>
> This art consisted of four successive stages, though there were only two commands: 1. *Mutzen ab!* 2. *Mutzen auf!* or "Caps off," "Caps on." But each command was divided into two separate tempos, hence the four stages and the strict, irrevocable protocol connected with them:

1. *Mutzen* . . . The right hands rose up to the caps and waited motionlessly . . .

2. . . . *ab!* . . . hands snatched off the caps and with a synchronous, loud clap like the crack of a whip, slapped them against the right thighs.

3. *Mutzen* . . . Hands went up, clumsily set caps on heads, and again waited . . .

4. . . . *auf!* . . . hands went down, this time without the caps, palms slapping against the right thighs with the same synchronous and loud-as-possible crack.

Only then could one freely adjust one's cap to be ready for a repetition of the ritual.

Try this on several hundred worn-out, starving, thirsty human beings hardly standing on their feet and you can imagine how much time it takes to learn this art, or rather to learn it imperfectly. (pp. 24–25)

At times individual voices also reveal a particular humanity and subversion of the deadly rationality of Auschwitz. In Nomberg-Przytyk's tale, there is a "Catch 22": the SS had determined that newborns who survived their arduous births at Auschwitz were to be killed along with their mothers. To save the mothers, the women delivered in secrecy. Women from the infirmary suffocated the newborn or gave it a lethal injection before it took its first breath. "The mother is told that the baby was born dead" (p. 69). A woman named Esther resists this cruel logic. She plays the role of the naive "fool" who does not comprehend–who resists the world as it presents itself to her and "makes strange" (to use Bakhtin's phrase, 1981, p. 402) its practice.[11] Esther believed–as perhaps all mothers do–that her child would be too beautiful for anyone to kill, and gives birth to a son in the infirmary. With great pride and delight she nurses him. On the third day, an SS physician, Josef Mengele,[12] arrives at the infirmary and, without a second thought, sends Esther and her splendid baby to their deaths. "She went naked, and in her arms she held the baby. She held it up high as though she wanted to show them what a beautiful and healthy son she had" (p. 71).[13]

While Nomberg-Przytyk and Fenelon often use the language of the reporter, they too know that much is ephemeral rumor. They speak in the language of hearsay: "it was said that" (Fenelon, p. 222), and "rumors were flying everywhere" (Nomberg-Przytyk, p. 8). Survivors' proximity to events often limited their perceptions—in fact, the "reality" of concentration camp inmates was easily manipulated and distorted by their captors.

LANGUAGE AND CULTURE

The first response to the Holocaust was stunned—and perhaps respectful—silence. There were no words—no language—suitable or even capable of representing its horrors, none that could describe what had happened. In spite of the richness of these stories, their language only encircles and approaches the events themselves; words stand in for memories. Lived chaos is always beyond words, and story-telling requires distance for reflection. For Delbo, memories of Auschwitz are nightmares beyond words. She captures the power of the word and imagery. Her deep physical and emotional memories of the Holocaust invade her consciousness as nightmarish sensations and images. In her latest publication, a 1985 collection of essays titled *Days and Memory* (beautifully translated from the French in 1990 by her friend Rosette Lamont), Delbo comments on her ability to speak of the Holocaust most clearly from a detached perspective:

> [W]hen I talk to you about Auschwitz, it is not from deep memory that my words issue. They come from external memory, . . . from intellectual memory, the memory connected with thinking processes. Deep memory preserves sensations, physical imprints. It is the memory of the senses. For it isn't words that are swollen with emotional charge. Otherwise, someone who has been tortured by thirst for weeks on end could never again say, "I'm thirsty. How about a cup of tea." This word has also split in two. Thirst has turned back into a word for commonplace use. But if I dream of the thirst I suffered in Birkenau, I once again see the person I was, haggard, halfway crazed, near to collapse; I physically feel that real thirst and it is an atrocious nightmare. If however, you'd like me to talk to you about it . . . (1990, pp. 3–4)

Delbo can and does use words to capture the nightmare reality of her experiences. But to do so, she departs from straightforward intellectual telling of the past, and focuses on one word, "thirst."

One reviewer summarized Delbo's story as an exploration of silence and language:

> One wonders with Charlotte Delbo just how it can mean anything that one has "survived a death camp" and so ponders the chilling question buried at the heart of her work . . . might it not have been better for the sake of coherence if no one had ever come back at all? (Kingcaid 1984, p. 108)

At times Delbo expresses her nightmarish memories as surrealistic theater, especially in *Days and Memory* (1990). Auschwitz is set apart from the rest of the world, but with all-too-real consequences. As a playwright, her writing is different from any other author in this study, male or female: at times poetic, at times starkly theatrical. Her narrative moves back and forth from past tense to present and back to past, weaving the fabric of her story as a re-lived and remembered memory. Delbo uses evocative symbols and exquisite imagery to convey complex stories and variegated meanings. As Langer described her writing, "the poetic style freezes the horror instead of transfiguring it . . . her language approaches the status of music with its lyric repetitions and incantations, though she seeks visual images equivalent to the rhythmic phrases of sound" (1978, p. 203).

With Auschwitz, all language is corrupt and ungrounded, stolen and slain. Amery has lost his "home and mother tongue" (p. 54). The word itself has died, for "the word always dies where the claim of some reality is total. It died for us a long time ago" (p. 20). There are not enough words left to rebuild home, language, and culture. At Auschwitz, Amery tells us, a poem could not "transcend reality" (p. 7).

Levi writes in a similar vein. At Auschwitz words are lost to blows, and with them is lost all claim to humanity. "This [the language of blows] was a signal: for those people we were no longer men" (1989, p. 91). The words that do survive are inadequate. Levi mourns the loss of meaning in the word:

> Just as our hunger is not that feeling of missing a meal, so our way of being cold has need of a new word. We say "hunger," we say "tiredness," "fear," "pain," we say "winter" and they are different things. They are free words, created and used by free men

who lived in comfort and suffering in their homes. If the Lagers[14] had lasted longer, a new harsh language would have been born; and only this language could express what it means to toil the whole day in the wind, with the temperature below freezing, wearing only a shirt, underpants, cloth jacket and trousers, and in one's body nothing but weakness, hunger and knowledge of the end drawing nearer. (1961, pp. 112–13)

Those who speak of the Holocaust have had to reinvent meanings for ordinary everyday words. Conventional language is inadequate at best. At its worst, it normalizes unprecedented suffering and places it within a continuity of history and experience. One word—one image—takes on new meanings: trains, camp, barbed wire, counting, selection, showers, gas, ovens, chimneys, ashes, hunger and thirst. Each brings a multitude of inexpressible associations to mind. The very words used to tell stories of the Holocaust have themselves become metaphors. Even the word "Holocaust" has become a metaphor for suffering that goes beyond words.[15] Each image shapes and, in turn, draws from texts of collective memory.

For novelist and essayist Norma Rosen, Holocaust imagery is dynamic.[16] It is alive today and invested with a second life that extends far beyond experiences of survivors and their families.

Trains and toilets, labor pains and hunger. For a mind engraved with the Holocaust, gas is always *that* gas. Shower means their shower. Ovens are those ovens. A train is a freight car crammed with suffocating children: it arrives at the suburban station in a burst of power and noise, there is a moment of hideous hallucination that is really only remembering, and then one steps into the train and opens the newspaper. . . . Of course this does not always happen. Some days the sky is simply blue and we do not wonder how a blue sky looked to those on their way to the crematoria. (1992, p. 52)

Laks explains, "Like most former camp inmates I avoid talks on these subjects as much as possible, for I get the impression that, except for the 'initiated,' I am talking with people who do not understand the language I am speaking to them" (p. 17). And for Nomberg-Przytyk, after liberation, there is an abyss of language and understanding between herself and the world: "I did not have the strength to talk, right now, just to satisfy someone's curiosity. . . . I listened, but the words did not make any sense to me. I was asked a question about something, but I did not answer. I simply could not speak" (p. 159).

Stories of the Holocaust that most effectively capture the violence and horror of its experienced reality frequently rely on metaphors, on words that speak to and beyond imagination, to awaken the senses rather than merely the rational intellect of comprehension. Between the Holocaust as event and the Holocaust as memory lays an abyss of untold complexity. The camp is hermetically sealed, a completely other world beyond descriptions useful for the world we know. Knowing full well that existing language is inadequate, they tell us that it was something like something we know, but qualitatively and quantitatively different, more all-encompassing than anything imaginable.

Within the stories, I found one metaphor that allows me to grapple with the commonalities and particularities of the stories: Auschwitz is not merely another world, it is a god-forsaken hell. Fenelon quotes Eva's description of Auschwitz as "the devil's cauldron" (p. 194). In his 1979 work, *Moments of Reprieve*, Levi likens Auschwitz to Dante's inferno. For Delbo, "Hell has vomited all its damned" (p. 134), but Auschwitz goes beyond the horrors of hell:

> *In hell*
>
> *you do not see your comrades dying*
>
> *in hell*
>
> *death is no threat*
>
> *you no longer feel hunger or thirst in hell*
>
> *you no longer await anything*
>
> *in hell*
>
> *there is no more hope*
>
> *and hope is anguish*
>
> *in the heart empty of blood.*
>
> *Why then do you say that it is hell,*
>
> *here. (p. 134)*

While Amery uses metaphors of Auschwitz as an "Inferno" (p. 12) or "hell" (p. 35), and himself as one of the "resurrected"

(p. 64) or a Kafkaesque "bug" (p. 64), he also experienced Auschwitz as intense and unremitting reality. "Nowhere else in the world did reality have as much effective power as in the camp, nowhere else was reality so real. In no other place did the attempt to transcend it prove so hopeless and so shoddy" (p. 19).

Later, without claiming any possibility of redemption through suffering, Amery continues, "even in direct experience everyday reality is nothing but codified abstraction. Only in rare moments of life do we truly stand face to face with the event and with it, reality" (p. 26). Using the Christian metaphor of crucifixion, he writes of the immutability of Auschwitz, "It nails every one of us onto the cross of his ruined past" (p. 68).[17]

Not only the word, but all culture and all means of communication join in the macabre contortion of Auschwitz. Fenelon tells us of one evening when the women give a concert in the women's infirmary, knowing that their audience will be gassed the next morning. Fenelon finds irony in the performance and the orchestra's choice of works–from "The Blue Danube" to "Land of Smiles." For the audience, the music is torment beyond endurance: "Some shrieked like suffering animals, some . . . blocked their ears, rocked in time. Some oblivious to our presence, were praying, hands clasped. Very few were following the concert in the normal fashion" (p. 128). When the concert is over, Fenelon wonders how she could have brought such pain to her comrades: "Had we already become brutes? How could one explain one's indifference?" (p. 130). She no longer knows who she is. Clara is not alone torturing other prisoners on behalf of the SS.

Laks tells of a similar scene in the women's infirmary. On Christmas eve the men begin a concert with a gentle rendition of "Silent Night." But the musicians move quickly from *piano* to *fortissimo* as the women's sobs threaten to drown out their music. "From all sides spasmodic cries, ever more numerous, ever shriller . . . began to roll in on me: 'Enough of this! Stop! Begone! Clear out! Let us croak in peace!'" (p. 99).

Allying himself with the SS in their love of music, Laks has risen through the hierarchy of Auschwitz. At times he seems to care more for the quality of music at Auschwitz than for the musicians. But he cannot be so easily dismissed. He borrows the rationality of the Germans, and knows full well what he is doing. As Kapellmeister, he knows that his German superiors have no concern for the health and well-being of his musicians. Laks knows all too well that the SS do not expect him to survive Auschwitz: He is neither their peer nor their colleague—merely a pleasant diversion to be exploited. He too recognizes the absurdity of music at Auschwitz, yet hopes that his writing

> . . . may even introduce a few new contradictions. Is not one of them the very fact that music—that most sublime expression of the human spirit—also became entangled in the hellish enterprise of the extermination of millions of people and even took an active part in this extermination? (p. 5)

For Amery, all cultural heritage is shattered. In his lament over the upside-down world of Auschwitz, Amery begins with his narrow definition of the intellectual as one like himself. He has not so much lost his cultural heritage as had it stolen by inferior Germans who have less right to it than he: "In Auschwitz, however, the isolated individual had to relinquish all of German culture, including Durer and Reger, Gryphius and Trakl, to even the lowest SS man" (p. 8). As Amery's chilling words tell us, the "bureaucrats of torture" have within their power the ability to destroy the human repositories of culture: "A slight pressure by the tool-wielding hand is enough to turn the other—along with his head, in which are perhaps stored Kant and Gehel, and all nine symphonies, and the World as Will and Representation—into a shrilly squealing piglet at slaughter" (p. 35).

The survivors whose stories I've been reading were all intellectuals. Their knowledge and skills could earn them privileges, but also contempt.[18] Survivors disallow the comfort I wish for in imagining that disproportionately more intellectuals survived, were treated better, or "survived better or died with more dignity" (Amery 1977, p. 13). In a 1986 interview with Levi, Philip Roth attempts to credit Levi's "professional character" and "systematic mind" with his survival. Levi refuses to acquiesce, and responds: "I insist there was no general rule, except entering the camp in good health and knowing German. Barring this, luck dominated" (p. 180).

Events of Auschwitz and their storied representations stand in unresolved tension. Themes of overwhelming aesthetic and moral difficulties of representation are juxtaposed with moral imperatives to represent and remember the multitude of voices giving witness and expression to the horror of this event. For Auschwitz and its representation, this problem is particularly difficult: there is a great chasm of inexpressibility. For survivors, and even more for those of us removed by time and distance, chaos overwhelms our stories and truths lie beyond our tellings.

My thoughts on chaos and the grotesque echo Hannah Arendt's writings on totalitarianism, evil, and the violence that permeated every aspect of life and death at Auschwitz. Arendt places Auschwitz in the center of the brutal ideology of the Nazi regime. Grotesque violence emerges as the essence of Auschwitz's institutional organization. In Auschwitz irrationality and chaos are juxtaposed with cruel bureaucratic logic.[19]

At times the voices from Auschwitz reveal a particular humanity and subversion of the deadly rationality of Auschwitz. Resistance to total domination demands that the particular be celebrated, not incorporated into a single story or grand narrative. "Total domination. . . strives to organize the infinite plurality and differentiation of human beings as if all of humanity were just one individual. . . . Totalitarian domination seeks to achieve this goal through . . . absolute terror in the camps" (Arendt 1973, p. 438). For me the multiple stories and truths come closer to conveying the lived experiences of chaos at Auschwitz than would any single voice or omniscient chronicle. Sadly and too often, as in the story of Esther, resistance is deadly and only possible in the guise of the fool. My third reading is an attempt to show that Auschwitz was a place of chaos and loss, of annihilation of the categories by which humans situate themselves and understand their worlds. The more I read and thought of Auschwitz, the more its grotesque chaos came to the fore. I'd learned that I couldn't neatly grasp Auschwitz nor even its survivors' stories. This reading reminds me that Auschwitz was real, and that its sinister rationality, stories of hideous degradation, language, and even humor were unequivocally evil.

NOTES

[1]. Other Auschwitz survivors write of maintaining aspects of their pre-camp identity through their trades. For example, physicians Elie Cohen (1973), Miklos Nyiszli (1978), and Gisela Perl (1984) practiced medicine in the camps. Olga Lengyel (1947), a medical student, functioned as a physician at Auschwitz. Fania Fenelon and Szymon Laks maintained occupational continuity as musicians at Auschwitz.

[2]. The title of Sutzkever's remarkable collection of poems, "Burned Pearls," is redolent of Molodowsky's "gold encrusted chaos."

[3]. See David K. Danow's (1995) analysis of Bakhtinian notions of the carnivalesque-grotesque in which he includes several Holocaust texts.

[4]. There has been much debate over if and how the Holocaust was historically unique. I believe that it was, but I wish to shift our attention to the ways in which inmates of its work and death camps experienced the Holocaust as inimical to the narrative webs of their earlier lives.

[5]. Many titles of Holocaust fiction and memoirs use these metaphors as well. Examples include Saul Bellow's *Mr. Sammler's Planet* (1970), Elie Cohen's *The Abyss* (1973), Dov Edelstein's *Worlds Torn Asunder* (1984), Otto Frederick's *The Kingdom of Auschwitz* (1994), Wieslaw Kielar's *Anus Mundi* (1980), Judith Newman's *In the Hell of Auschwitz* (1963), and Cynthia Ozick's *The Cannibal Galaxy* (1983).

[6]. To use sociological jargon, Auschwitz was a total institution, strictly regimented and isolated from the rest of the world (Goffman, 1961).

[7]. In Auschwitz memoirs by Olga Lengyel (1947) and Filip Muller (1979), expectations of protection for women and children granted a sense of false security.

[8]. Gerald E. Markle (see his 1995 *Meditations of a Holocaust Traveler*, with a working title of "The Gray Zone") has added much to my understanding of the moral complexities of the Holocaust.

[9]. See Charlie Chaplin's 1940 movie "The Great Dictator" for a biting parody of Hitler and Nazi society.

[10]. In Markle's *Meditations of a Holocaust Traveler* he argues that this bed-making ritual captures the essence of the Holocaust, in which "[w]hat the Germans wanted, and what they got, was order and control amidst chaos and death" (1995, p. 6).

[11]. The image of the fool is pivotal in Bakhtin's discussions of discourse, and interacts with that of the "gay deception" of rogue. "Between the rogue and the fool there emerges, as a unique coupling of the two, the image of the clown. He is a rogue who dons the mask of a fool in order to motivate distortions and shufflings of languages and labels, thus unmasking them by not understanding them. . . . turning them inside out" (1981, pp. 404, 405).

[12]. According to Joan Ringelheim (1994), most Auschwitz survivors who mention a male physician at Auschwitz will speak of him as "Mengele."

Since there were over a dozen German physicians at Auschwitz, Ringelheim suspects individual memories have been shaped by well-publicized reports of Mengele's cruelty there. Mengele has, perhaps, become a synecdoche for Auschwitz physicians and the perversion of medicine.

13. This story is perhaps the best known of Nomberg's tales, and has been published separately by Amor Fati (Austin) in 1985 as *Esther's First Born.* The name Esther echoes that of the Biblical Queen Esther who defied her husband King Ahasuerus, and saved her Jewish nation from destruction. I've come across no stories by the women whose babies were killed at birth.

14. Throughout most of his writing, Levi uses the German word "Lager" to refer to the Nazi concentration camps. Not only individual words, but the camps themselves cannot be translated.

15. See Sylvia Plath's controversial poem "Daddy" (1962) for an example of aspects of the Holocaust (in this case Nazis) being used as metaphors for cruelty.

16. Not a survivor, Rosen writes in a collection of essays, *Accidents of Influence: Writing as a Woman and a Jew in America* (1992) and in her novel *Touching Evil* (1969) of how the Holocaust has contaminated all of life.

17. There are important limitations to the metaphor of Auschwitz as Hell. The analogy breaks down with a misleading–and, I would add, obscene–connotation of Hell (and thus the Holocaust) as divine punishment (particularly on the Jews). See Rubenstein (1992) for a critical discussion of situations in which both Jews and Gentiles have defined the Holocaust as a just punishment of the Jews sent by God. However, as noted by Arendt and others, the essential innocence of the victims was central to the ideology and practice of extermination.

18. Here I include physicians, musicians, writers rather than Amery's admittedly narrow definition of an intellectual as "a person who lives within what is a spiritual frame of reference in the widest sense. His realm of thought is an essentially humanistic one, that of the liberal arts. He has a well-developed aesthetic consciousness. By instinct and ability he tends toward abstract trains of thought" (1977, p. 2).

19. While chaos and a sense of profound unreality permeate all personal testimony, I do not concur with Arendt's (1973) claim that therefore survivors' stories cannot lead *toward* understanding.

CHAPTER 6

Reflections

> *You all remember Adorno's dictum that it is barbaric to write poetry after Auschwitz . . . [T]hen is it not equally barbaric to write footnotes after Auschwitz?*
>
> —Hilberg 1988, p. 25

Journal Entry: April 24, 1996

The Van Andel Public Museum of Grand Rapids, Michigan, is showing "Rescuers of the Holocaust." The curators have supplemented the original fifty-six portraits and stories with seven of "West Michigan Rescuers." Grand Rapids is a religious center for the Dutch Calvinist community in North America. Each of the West Michigan rescuers is from the Netherlands. Although the exhibition is co-sponsored by the Jewish Community Fund of Grand Rapids, this Holocaust story, one with which the citizens of West Michigan can most closely identify, is a story of non-Jews. It presents very little information about the Holocaust itself, and describes itself as:

> An exhibition focusing on the people who resisted Hitler's attempts at genocide by saving Jews during World War II, including a local component featuring rescuers who have immigrated to West Michigan.

The Exhibit flier includes a $1.00 coupon for the film "Anne Frank Remembered" which is also showing in Grand Rapids. *Discoveries*, the newsletter for "Friends of the Public Museum," highlights the stories of the seven with a front page article, "Risking Their Lives to Rescue the Innocent." A press release from the museum tells readers, "The perpetrators of the Holocaust and the six million Jews they murdered are far better known than the few who risked their lives to save others during that barbaric time."

A large open book is half-filled with museum visitors' responses to the question, "Are these people heros?" The rescuers deny that they are heros, but few agree with them. Many of the responses are by children who had come to the museum on class trips. A group of children, perhaps fourth graders like my younger son, are trying to make connections between what they see and what they know from their lives.

> Student: *Look at all these old people. They're even older than my grandparents. What did they do?*
>
> Tour Guide: *They rescued Jews during the Holocaust.*
>
> Student: *When was that?*
>
> Tour Guide: *During World War II, over fifty years ago.*
>
> Students: *My grandpa flew an army plane in a war.*
>
> *Did he bomb anything?*
>
> *Of course.*
>
> *My dad was in the Vietnam War.*
>
> Teacher: *Let's look at the rest of the pictures, and see what we can learn.*
>
> Students: *Look, they have old fashioned pictures of these people and their families when they were young.*
>
> *They have really weird clothes.*
>
> *Do you think these people were bombed?*
>
> *Maybe they rescued people whose houses were bombed.*
>
> *It says they rescued Jews. Maybe they rescued Jewish pilots who were shot down by the enemy.*
>
> *Who was the enemy?*
>
> *Why are there only pictures of people who rescued Jews? Didn't anyone else get bombed?*
>
> Tour Guide: *Many people were bombed and killed, but Hitler tried to kill all the Jews, that's what the Holocaust means.*
>
> Students: *Did they kill kids too?*
>
> Tour Guide: *Yes, they killed millions of Jews, including children.*
>
> Students: *I'm glad we fought the war to rescue the Jews. My grandpa should have his picture here.*

The Rescuers' Exhibit brings me back to one of my starting points: How do people today come to know about the Holocaust? What should they know? In these portraits and in stories, lives of people who were there can touch the lives of us who were not. I hope these children have already been introduced to some who needed rescuing. Do they know that there were far too few rescuers? The stories of the survivors and victims numerically far surpasses those of the rescuers. Through their written words seven survivors and one victim have taken leading roles as my teachers. During months of re-reading their stories, I've had to begin with what was familiar to me—differences in gender, sociological categories of identity—before I could approach the anti-narrative chaos that permeates their words. At times I've turned to rescuers' stories to balance those of victims, survivors, and perpetrators, to anchor myself outside the absolute horror and remind myself that possibilities for human courage and goodness endure.

SITUATED CHOICES

I began this intellectual and personal story with choices about what to read and how. Although I claim to celebrate the particularity of voices, I have followed some of the dictates of canon. Each work discussed in this book has passed the hurdles of publication and translation into English. I have chosen well-articulated stories over those whose style mimics the chaos and confusion of Auschwitz.[1] I have chosen works within the public domain that most clearly address my research interests and seem appropriate to multiple readings. I have been especially drawn to those women's voices and to non-heroic male voices that dare to look chaos in its face, that do not demand restitution for their suffering.

I'm often asked why I have chosen to speak here only of published stories of survivors. Why not oral testimony? Why not personal interviews? Why not dictated stories, oral stories meant for inscription? I'm grateful to British sociologist Bogusia Temple for one answer. She argues against privileging interview data and oral life accounts over written accounts. While oral and written accounts are structurally distinct and demand different tools of analysis, I do not find either genre more authentic, more valid, or closer to lived truths than the other. Written accounts demand attention to layout, punctuation, and processes of publication. Oral texts are shaped more by tone and pitch. But the differences are more in degree rather than in kind. "Both are 'performances' for different audiences, neither of which can 'capture' a life" (Temple 1994, p. 39).

Choices about how to read have been more difficult than those about what to read. The three-readings framework is of course artificial. Early on, when I found myself reading and re-reading the stories, I organized my notes into three piles, confidentially labeled dialectical inquiries: thesis, antithesis, and synthesis or anti-synthesis. Later, I dropped the labels as too pretentious and optimistic, but kept the three-part frame, positing each reading as a necessary prelude to the next. I could now construct an orderly tale about my three readings:

> I have chosen to write about reading Auschwitz survivor stories within a structure of multiple readings, in hopes that my telling reflects and illustrates something of the multiplicity of stories and partial truths of Auschwitz. Each reading is necessary; each reveals different truths. They are necessarily sequential, building upon each other and bringing me closer to understanding something of the lived experiences of these survivors. This understanding is balanced with a growing awareness that I can never fully comprehend others' lived experiences, especially those of chaos and horror. Each reading enters into a dialogic encounter with each other reading and with me, a reader. Collectively, they speak across and within gendered spaces as polyphonic voices of a larger Holocaust text and have become characters in my life story.
>
> Two exemplary Holocaust characters set the stage for this story: one, Anne Frank, a female victim, and the other, Elie Wiesel, a male survivor. Their stories are undoubtedly the best-known Holocaust stories in the United States, and were pivotal in my own initial awareness of the Holocaust. Each speaks of the overwhelming de-humanization of Auschwitz, and each is metonymical—allowing access of a whole through multiple yet particular interconnected fragments (Young 1991, p. 303). The particular resonates with the whole.
>
> However, when I closely read other particular stories about Auschwitz I found that Frank and Wiesel don't always work as composite characters. Their stories are not only universal, but also particular, two out of many. The number of personal Auschwitz

stories grows every year, adding less often heard stories, very different from Frank's and Wiesel's.[2] We cannot change the past nor its stories, but, in Judith Fetterley's words, "we can accurately name the reality they do reflect and so change literary criticism from a closed conversation to an active dialogue" (1978, p. xxiii).[3] Bakhtin's writings have framed my thoughts on the universal and the particular in Auschwitz stories. The notion of a single representative or story simultaneously claims a false and a genuine universality. The dialogic, at both dichotomous and multi-voiced levels, highlights the particular. With notions of cacophony, we circle back to the universal and the particular.

In Chapter Three I addressed the need to hear more Auschwitz stories and contrasted writings by female and male survivors, looking for patterned differences. This reading, using a two-dimensional, rather primitive feminist template, confirmed gendered expectations. I found what I was looking for. Women's stories of their experiences and concerns were often different from their male counterparts. Themes of mutual support and reproductive anxieties resonate throughout these women's stories.

But again, there was more; a close reading revealed too many exceptions. The gendered pairs lost their initial tidy boundaries that worked so well in a two-dimensional reading. Dichotomous categories are inherently simplistic—essentialist. An essentializing gendered reading suggests that there is one essential and collective voice for women of the death camps and another for men. On reflection, this reading left me thinking of survivor stories as static documents rather than vibrant discourses, and I glossed over the collected particularity of these and other less powerful voices. While necessary for correcting over-reliance on a representative male survivor story and a female victim story, a two-dimensional template did not sufficiently account for other patterns.

I read the stories again, expanding my template to include categories such as nationality, ethnicity, ideology, and status. I found textual support for this framework as well. I congratulated myself. I could now interweave gender with complexities of individual and collective identities. This reading not only captured more of the stories' richness, but was truer to ways in which survivors re-claimed and re-created identities for themselves within Auschwitz. Furthermore, a multidimensional template encouraged me to listen more closely to their words. I could now argue for the situated complexity of all survivor stories.

Left to itself, my first reading lends itself to stereotyped, essentialist thought. If I add a "women's voice" from Auschwitz, I risk telling merely another master narrative, that of women survivors as heroic "Other," subsuming their voices into a single story, and leaving male stories center-stage.[4] Any dichotomous gendered categories, including my pairing method of comparing female and male voices, reinforces a totalizing essentialism.[5] Master narratives neutralize and suppress ideologies, histories, and subjectivities non-identical to those of the universal human subject. The life stories of many people whose history differs from that of the universal human subject because of race, class, and gender identifications go unwritten, or if written, misread or unread (Smith 1993, p. 394).[6]

Any dichotomous analysis of "Other" reinforces ideologies of domination. Although much of the literature on gender and the Holocaust echoes dichotomy of practical and instrumental reasoning or private and public spheres, these categories are inherently ideological and counter-factual, firmly grounded in gendered subtexts. As such, they frequently mask implicit androcentric biases (Fraser 1989, pp. 8–9, 113–143). "Any universalized concept of 'woman'" is, in Smith's words, "inadequate" (1993, p. 397). I learned the necessity of honoring the particular, of reclaiming the oppositional voices of resistance to totalizing narratives.

While in my second reading I highlighted dangers of an essentialist gendered reading of Auschwitz stories, I do not wish to discount my first reading. The warp of the entire tapestry of my reading is the influence of gender on lived experiences and stories. Nonetheless, focusing exclusively on these patterns limits my understanding of the truths and richness of their stories. A gendered reading is strongest not when it ignores other strands of survivors' narratives, but when it weaves them into non-essentialist tellings and re-tellings of their stories.

After this reading, I still felt there was more. I was further removed from understanding survivors' experiences than before. With an indifferent scalpel, I'd dissected and classified survivors' words. I'd presented an order belied by the stories themselves.

The third reading of Chapter Five was an attempt to name and show that the stories cried out of chaos and loss, of annihilation of the categories by which humans situate themselves and understand their worlds. The more I read and thought of Auschwitz, the more its grotesque chaos comes to the fore. I'd learned that I couldn't neatly grasp Auschwitz nor even its survivors' stories. In writing Chapter V, some of my own anchors worked loose from their moorings: moral end points, rationality, language itself.

Unfortunately for my intellectual peace of mind, this how-I-read-Auschwitz-stories tale does not hold its center. Even the terms "the dialogic" and "the grotesque" all too easily point toward redemptive potentials. Bakhtin's notion of the grotesque is closely tied to the notion of carnival, with its temporary challenges and ultimate return to pre-existing social relations. At Auschwitz the stakes were much higher—for those who died, for those who survived, and for humanity. Not only have I remained unable to tuck in the loose ends of each telling or tell a story that I knew was true for me, but the readings refuse to step aside for each other. All three jostle for dominance as they co-exist: simultaneous, discordant, incompatible narratives. With their absolute and blatant refusal to stay within categories of organization and understanding, survivor stories will not let me pretend that two- or even multidimensional understandings of any story are adequate. Presenting the readings sequentially tells a story of coming closer to an authentic reading, but ignores the fact that each reading becomes more emotionally intolerable. It is true that each reading is an attempt to go beyond the previous one, but it is untrue to suggest that each one replaces or merely builds on prior ones. The writing process itself makes this impossible—my re-writes do not occur in linear fashion. The grotesque reality of Auschwitz threatens to define all reality if I stay with it too long; so I hold onto touchstones from my other readings: women supporting each other, courage, ethnic cohesiveness, cultural resources. Otherwise, Auschwitz spills over into my everyday lived stories. It is less wholly other than an extreme of what holds for all experience: mediated tellings, narrative inaccessibility, potential for meaninglessness.

All words, stories, and readings belie the inexpressibility of lived experiences. Some survivors have chosen silence rather than risk having their lives and memories cannibalized by readers who were not there, who will never understand, never know. Fortunately, many survivors have not kept silence. They have told and re-told their stories of Auschwitz, directly and indirectly. Some, such as Delbo, Amery, Levi, and Wiesel have devoted their lives to writing their stories, essays, poetry, drama, and fiction. They cannot not speak. The stories of Auschwitz demand telling and re-telling, so that we may hear and re-hear. Melding her tales with visual imagery, Delbo said of her audiences, "They must be made to see" (in Langer 1995, p. x). Amery wrote that after writing an initial essay on intellectuals at Auschwitz, "suddenly everything demanded telling" (p. xix). He continues:

> [I] can do no more than give testimony . . . What occupies me, and what I am qualified to speak about, is the victims of this Reich. I don't want to erect a monument to them, for to be a victim is not an honor. I only wanted to describe their condition, which is unchangeable. (p. xviii)

Primo Levi also describes his stories, particularly his earlier ones, as testimony:

> At Auschwitz, and on the long road returning home, I had seen and experienced things that appeared important not only for me, things that imperiously demanded to be told. And I had told them, I had testified. (1979, p. 9)

At the end of a long career of writing and re-writing the stories of Auschwitz, Levi borrowed lines from Coleridge's "Ryme of the Ancient Mariner," telling us:

> "Until my ghastly tale is told
> This heart within me burns." (1989)

While I too write, I do so as a reader and a witness to survivors' stories. I have grown very fond of the survivors whose stories I am re-telling. I am grateful to them for making their stories known. John Ciardi's words, written of poet and Dachau survivor Josef Stein in "The Gift," ring true:

> clean white paper waiting under a pen
> is the gift beyond history and hurt and heaven. (1959, p. 65)

NOTES

[1]. For example the confusion of Auschwitz and of life after liberation are strikingly reflected in Elie A. Cohen's 1973 work, *The Abyss: A Confession.* Cohen, a Dutch Jew, worked as a prison-doctor at Auschwitz from September 1943 through January 1945. His wife and four-year-old son were murdered in the gas chambers there.

[2]. Writing from within the literary community, Smith (1993) offers general strategies which feminist biographers and autobiographers have used to "challenge official histories, including that of the universal human subject" (p. 394). Several, however, leave the "certitudes of bourgeois

individualism" (p. 395) intact, as does a dialogic analysis. One may, for example, give what Liz Stanley calls "contrasting exemplars" (1993, p. 46) of women who reject their given roles and challenge culturally approved modes of being and discourse.

3. See Yael Feldman's (1992) "Whose Story is it Anyhow?" for a discussion of how the particular and the subjective work against historical closure and tyrannical collective ideology.

4. Horkheimer and Adorno's warnings against subsumption anticipate arguments of poststructuralists against dominant master narratives (1974). Holocaust scholars have looked to the works of Jean-Francois Lyotard for insights into modernity, narrative and memory in light of the Holocaust (Hartman 1993; Huyssen 1993; Langer 1993).

5. Some scholars, such as Gabriel Mayotola (1995), have argued that women in concentration camps half a century ago were harder to humiliate than men because they were more used to being subservient.

6. See also Bauer (1991), Herndl (1991), Stevenson (1991), and Wills (1991) for similar arguments.

Appendix

BOOK-LENGTH PUBLISHED MEMOIRS OF AUSCHWITZ
Available in English

Abraham, Ben. 1996. *And the World Remained Silent.* New York: Vantage Press.

Abraham, Berndt. 1994. *No Graves to Visit: A Survivor Remembers at Last.* Larchmont, New York: Berndt Abraham Memorial Fund of Larchmeot Temple.

Adelsberger, Lucie. 1995. *Auschwitz: A Doctor's Story.* Boston: Northeastern University Press.

Adler, Sinai. 1996. *Your Rod and Your Staff: A Young Man's Chronicle of Survival.* Jerusalem; New York: Feldheim Publishers.

Amery, Jean. (1976) 1990. *At the Mind's Limits.* Translated by Sidney Rosenfeld and Stella P. Rosenfeld. New York: Schocken Books.

Arad, Dan. 1993. *How to Survive Auschwitz: 161205.* S.L.: D. Arad.

Barlev, Zvi. 1991. *Would God it were Night: The Ordeal of a Jewish boy From Cracow–Through Auschwitz, Mathausen, and Gusen.* New York: Vantage Press.

Benisch, Pearl. 1991. *To Vanquish the Dragon.* Jerusalem; New York: Feldman Publishers.

Bernstein, Sara Tuvel. 1997. *The Seamstress: A Memoir of Survival.* New York: G. P. Putnam's Sons.

Biderman, Cyle Oniman. 1990. *74233.* Chicago: Limud Foundation.

Birenbaum, Halina. 1971. *Hope is the Last to Die.* New York: Twayne.

Blumenstein, Lili Wider. 1990. *Lili.* New York: Shengold.

Brewster, Eva. 1994. *Progeny of Light: Vanished in Darkness.* Revised edition of (1984, 1986) *Vanished in Darkness: An Auschwitz Memoir.* 2nd ed. Edmonton: NeWest Press.

Cohen, Elie A. (1971) 1973. *The Abyss: A Confession.* Translated from the Dutch by James Brockway. New York: Norton.

Cohen, Gilles. 1992. *Tatooed Numbers in the Camps of Auschwitz-Birkenau.* New York: Sons and Daughters of Jewish French Deportees; Beate Klarsfeld Foundation.

Cyran, Henry. B. 1984. *Inside Auschwitz, Written in Blood: A Personal Memory.* Brookvales, N. S. W., Australia: Child and Henry.

Czelny, K. T. 1996. *My Journey from Auschwitz to Buckingham Palace.* London: K. T. Czelny.

Delbo, Charlotte. (1965) 1968. *None of Us Will Return.* Translated from the French (Aucum de nous ne Reviendra). Boston: Beacon

_____. (1985) 1990 *Days and Memory.* Translated and with a Preface by Rosette Lamont. (La Memoire et les Jours). Marlboro, Vermont: The Marlboro Press.

_____. 1997. *Convoy to Auschwitz: Women of the French Resistance.* Boston: Northeastern University Press.

Drecki, Zbignie. 1990. *Freedom and Justice: Spring from the Ashes of Auschwitz.* Exmouth, Devon: Z. Drecki.

Edelstein, Dov. 1984. *Worlds Torn Asunder.* New York: Ktav.

Elias, Ruth. 1998. *Triumph of Hope: From Theresienstadt and Auschwitz to Israel.* New York: John Wiley & Sons.

Faber, David. 1997. *Because of Romek: A Holocaust Survivor's Memoir.* El Cajon, CA: Granite Hills Press.

Fenelon, Fania. (1977) 1979. *The Musicians of Auschwitz.* Translated from French by Judith Landry (Sursis pour l'orchestre). London: Joseph. London: Sphere.

_____. *Playing for Time.* 1976, 1977, 1981, 1997. Translated from French by Judith Landry (Sursis pour l'orchestre). ed Fania Fenelon with Marcelle Routier; New York: Atheneum. London: Sphere. Syracuse, N.Y.: Syracuse University Press.

Frankel, Neftal. 1991. *I Survived Hell: The Testimony of a Survivor of the Nazi Extermination camps (Prisioner Number 161040).* Translated from the Spanish by Sergo Duarte (*Yo he conocido el infierno*). Preface by Yehuda Bauer. New York: Vantage Press.

Frankl, Victor. 1963. *Man's Search for Meaning.* Translated from the German (Ein Psycholog erlebt das Konzentrationslager, 1946); *From Death Camp to Existentialism: A Psychiatrist's Path to a New Therapy* (1959 in US).

Fried, Heidi. 1990. *Fragments of a Life: The Road to Auschwitz.* London: Hale.

Friedrich, Otto. 1994, 1996. *The Kingdom of Auschwitz.* New York: Harper Perennial, London: Penguin.

Furth, Valerie Jakober. 1989. *Cabbages & Geraniums: Memories of the Holocaust.* Boulder, New York: Social Science Monographs: Distributed by Columbia University Press.

Gelissen, Rena Kornreich. 1995. *Rena's Promise: A Story of Sisters in Auschwitz.* Boston: Beacon Press.

Geve, Thomas. 1987. *Guns and Barbed Wire: A Child Survives the Holocaust.* Chicago: Academy Chicago. (later edition of *Youth in Chains*)

_____. *Youth in Chains.* 1958; 2nd pocket bk ed. 1981. Jerusalem: R. Mass.

Glas-Larsson, Margareta. 1991. *I Want to Speak: The Tragedy and Banality of Survival in Terezin and Auschwitz.* Translated by Lowell Bangerter (Ich will reden). Riverside California: Ariadne Press (Studies in Austrian literature, culture & thought). Edited and Annotated by Gerhard Botz; assisted by Anton Pleimer & Harald Wildfellner; foreword by Bruno Creisky.

Goldberg, Izaak. 1978. *The Miracles Versus Tyranny.* New York: Philosophical Library.

Greenman, Leon. 1996. *Leon Greenman, Auschwitz Survivor 98288: A Resource for Holocaust Education.* London: The Jewish Museum.

Harshalom, Avraham. 1990. *Alive From the Ashes.* Translated by Peretz Kidron. (*Hayim min ha-efer*). Tel Aviv: Milo.

Hart, Kitty. (1981, 1982, 1983) 1985. *Return to Auschwitz: The Remarkable Story of a Girl Who Survived the Holocaust.* New York: Atheneum.

Heimler, Eugene. 1961. *Concentration Camp.* New York: Phyamid (original title *Night of the Mist*)

Hersh, Gizelle, and Peggy Mann. 1980. *Gizelle, Save the Children!* New York: Everest House.

Hyatt, Felicia B. 1991. *Close Calls: The Autobiography of a Survivor.* New York: Holocaust Library.

Isaacson, Judith Magyar. (1990) 1991. *Seed of Sarah: Memoirs of Survivor.* 2nd ed. Urbana: University of Illinois Press.

Isacovici, Salo. 1997. *Man of Ashes.* Lincoln: University of Nebraska Press.

Jackson, Livia. 1997. *I Have Lived a Thousand Years: Growing up in the Holocaust.* New York: Simon and Schuster Books for Young Readers.

Jacobs, Benjamin. 1995. *The Dentist of Auschwitz: A Memoir.* Lexington: University Press of Kentucky.

Jani, Emilio. 1961. *My Voice Saved Me: Auschwitz 180046.* Translated from the Italian by Timothy Paterson. (*Mi ha salvato la voce*). Milano: Centauro Editrice.

Ka-tzetnik. 135633. 1989. *Shivitti: A Vision.* Translated from the Hebrew by Eliyah Nike De-Nur and Lisa Herman (*Tsofen*). San Francisco: Harper & Row.

Kellner, Tana. 1992. *B 11226, Fifty Years of Silence: Eugene Kellner's Story.* Rosendale, New York: Women's Studio Workshop.

Kern, Alice. 1988. *Tapestry of Hope.* Cathedral City, California: Limited Edition Books.

Kessel, Sim. (1972, 1973) 1975. *Hanged at Auschwitz.* Briarcliff Manor, New York: Stein & Day. Translated from the French by Melville & Delight Wallace (*Pendu a Auschwitz*).

Kielar, Wieslaw. 1980. *Anus Mundi: Five Years in Auschwitz.* New York: Times Books.

Kimmelman, Mira Ryczke. 1997. *Echoes from the Holocaust: A Memoir.* Knoxville: University of Tennessee Press.

Kor, Eva Moses. 1995. *Echoes From Auschwitz: Dr. Mengele's Twins, The Story of Eva and Miriam Mozes.* Terre Haute, Indiana: Candles, Inc.

Krakowski, Avra. 1995. *Counterfeit Lives.* New York: C.I.S. Publishers.

Krawczyk, Josef Gustav. 1976. *Living in Hell: An Account of Three Years in Auschwitz.* Edited by Josef Gustav Krawczyk, with the assistance of Lavinia M. Hill. Farnham Common, Bucks.: Beacon Press.

Laks, Szymon. 1989. *Music of Another World.* Translated by Chester Kisiel (*Musizues d'un autre monde*). Evanston, Illinois: Northwestern University Press.

Lasker-Wallfisch, Anita. 1996. *Inherit the Truth, 1939–1945: The Documented Experiences of a Survivor of Auschwiz and Bergen-Belsen.* London: Giles de la Mare.

Leitner, Isabella. 1992. *The Big Lie: A True Story.* New York: Scholastic Inc.

_____. (1978) 1988. *Fragments of Isabella.* Edited by Isabella Leitner and Irving Leitner. With an epilogue by Irving Leitner. New York: Crowell.

_____. 1994. *Isabella: From Auschwitz to Freedom.* (edited merging of *Fragments of Isabella and Saving the Fragments*). New York: Anchor Books.

_____. 1985, 1986. *Saving the Fragments: From Auschwitz to New York.* New York: New American Library.

Lengyel, Olga. (1946) 1947. *I Survived Hitler's Ovens.* Original English title, *Five Chimneys: The Story of Auschwitz).* Translated from the Hungarian *(Souveniers de l'au-del'a, Memories from Beyond).* Chicago: Ziff-Davis.

Levi, Primo. (1988) 1989. *The Drowned and the Saved.* Translated from the Italian by Raymond Rosenthal *(Sommersi e i salvati).* New York: Summit Books.

_____. (1981) 1986. *Moments of Reprieve.* Translated from the Italian by Ruth Feldman (Lilit e altri Racconti - Lilith and other Tales). London: Abacus.

_____. (1975) 1984. *The Periodic Table.* Translated from the Italian by Raymond Rosenthal. (*Il Sistema Periodico*). New York: Schocken Books.

_____. (1963) 1965. *The Reawakening.* Translated by Stuart Woolf. New York: Collier Books.

_____. (1947, 1959) 1961. *Survival in Auschwitz: The Nazi Assault on Humanity.* Translated from the Italian *(Se questo 'e un uomo, If this is a Man).* New York: Collier.

Lewinska, Pelgia. (1945) 1968. *Twenty Months at Auschwitz.* Translated from the Polish (*Vingt mois 'a Auschwitz, Auschwitz: Shame and a Person's Triumph*).

Litomisky, Otak. 1970. *The Memories of Prisoner Number 113359: Auschwitz 113359, Buchenwald 16283, Dora 16283.* S.L.: O. Litomisky.

Lustigman, Michael. 1988. *Kindness and Truth and the Art of Reading Ashes.* New York: P. Lang. American University Studies, Series IX, History, vol 38.

Mechanicus, Philip. 1969. *Year of Fear: A Jewish Prisoner Waits for Auschwitz.* New York: Hawthorn Books.

Menasche, Albert. 1947. *Birkenau (Auschwitz II): Memories of an Eyewitness: How 72,000 Greek Jews Perished: by Albert Menasche, number 124,454.* New York: I. Saltiel.

Mermelstein, Mel. (1979) 1981. *By Bread Alone: The Story of A-4685.* 1979. Los Angeles: Crescent Publications. Huntington Beach, California: distributed by Auschwitz Study Foundation.

Millu, Liana. 1991. *Smoke over Birkenau.* Philadelphia: Jewish Publication Society.

Michel, Earnest. W. 1993. *Promises to Keep.* New York: Barricade Books.

Mirchuk, Petro. (1976) 1985. *In the German Mills of Death, 1941–1945.* 2nd edition. Washington, D.C.: Survivors of the Holocaust.

Muller, Filip. 1984. *Eyewitness Auschwitz: Three Years in the Gas Chambers.* Briarcliff, New York: Stein & Day.

_____. 1979. *Auschwitz Inferno: The Testimony of a Sonderkommando.* London: Routledge and Kegan Paul.

Nahon, Marco. 1989. *Birckenau: The Camp of Death.* Translated from the French by Jacqueline Havaux Bowers. (*Birkenau*). Edited and with an introduction by Steven Bowman. Tuscaloosa: University of Alabama Press. Judaic studies series.

Neray. Ruth Bindefeld. 1992. *Death by Design.* Toronto: Childe Thursday.

Newman, Judith Sternberg. (1963) 1978. *In the Hell of Auschwitz: The Wartime Memoirs of Judith Sternberg Newman.* New York: Exposition Press.

Niescior, Leon. 1956. *I Survived Hell on Earth.* New York: S.L.

Nomberg-Przytyk, Sara. 1990. *Esther's First Born.* Austin: Amor Fati.

_____. 1985. *Auschwitz: True Tales From a Grotesque Land.* Translated from an unpublished 1966 Polish manuscript by Roslyn Hirsch. Edited by Eli Pfefferkorn and David Hirsch. Chapel Hill: University of North Carolina Press.

Nyiszli, Miklos. (1960) 1978. *Auschwitz: A Doctor's Eye-Witness Account.* Translated from the Hungarian by Tibere Kremer and Richard Seaver (*Dr. Mengele boncoloorvosa voltam*). With a foreword by Bruno Bettelheim. London: Mayflower.

Perl, Gisella. 1984. *I Was A Doctor at Auschwitz.* Salem, N H: Ayer.

Piekarski, Konstanty R. 1989. *Escaping Hell: The Story of a Polish Underground Officer in Auschwitz and Buchenwald.* Toronto: Dundurn Press.

Raab, Elisabeth M. 1997. *And Peace Never Came.* Waterloo, Ont.: Wilfrid Laurier University Press.

Ramati, Alexander. 1986. *And the Violins Stopped Playing.*

Rosenberg, Carl. 1990. *As God is my Witness.* New York: Holocaust Library.

Rosicki, Tadeus. 1984. *My Fifty Months in Nazi Camps: The Message of Survival.* S.L.: T. Rosicki.

Rybak, Rywka. 1993. *Ryska Rybak: A Survivor of the Holocaust.* Cleveland, Ohio: Tricycle Press.

Sattler, Stanislaw. (1980) 1981. *Prisoner of 68 Months – Buchenwald & Auschwitz.* 2nd ed. Jerusalem: Republished by Stefen Sattler for his father: Gefen Publishing Company.

Schloss, Eve. 1988. *Eva's Story: A Survivor's Tale* (by the step-sister of Anne Frank, with Evelyn Julia Kent). London: W. H. Allen.

Sevillias, Errikos. 1983. *Athens, Auschwitz.* Athens, Greece: Lycabettus Press.

Shay, Arnold L. 1996. *From Bendzin to Auschwitz: A Journey to Hell.* Hanover, Massachusetts: The Christopher House.

Snap, Leah. 1993. *Hatikvah in Auschwitz.* Hafia: Lea Schnapp.

Stadler, Aranka. 1995. *Mosaics of a Nightmare.* Great Britain: Kall-Kwik Printing.

Strumah, Yaakov. 1996. *Violinist in Auschwitz: From Salonica to Jerusalem, 1913–1967.* Konstanz, Germany: Hartung-Gorre.

Szmaglewska, Seweryna. 1947. *Smoke over Birkenau.* New York: Holt

Tedeschi, Giuliana. 1992. *There is a Place on Earth: A Woman in Birkenau.* Translated by Tim Parks. New York: Pantheon.

Vrba, Rudolf and Alan Bestic. 1989. *44070: The Conspiracy of the Twentieth Century.* Bellingham, Washington: Star & Cross.

_____. 1968. *I Cannot Forgive.* New York: Bantam.

Weitz, Sonia Schreiber. 1993. *I Promised I Would Tell.* Brookline, MA: Facing History and Ourselves.

Wiesel, Elie. (1956, 1958) 1960. *Night.* Translated from the Yiddish (*Un di velt hot geshvign, The World was Silent*) and from the French. New York: Hill & Wang.

Wolfin, Rene. 1994. *Ashes and Remorse: Memoirs of Resistance and Deportation from Auschwitz to Dachau.* S.L.: Palavas Press.

Zyskind, Sara. 1989. *Struggle (Maavako shel naar).* Minneapolis: Lerner Publications.

_____. 1981. *Stolen Years.* Minneapolis: Lerner.

Zywulska, Krystyna. (1951) 1957. *I Came Back.* Boston: Brown Watson.

References

Adorno, Theodor W. 1973. *Negative Dialectics*, translated by E. B. Ashton. New York: Seabury Press.

Amery, Jean. (1976) 1990. *At the Mind's Limits*, translated by Sidney Rosenfeld and Stella P. Rosenfeld. New York: Schocken Books.

———. 1964. *Preface to the Future: Culture in a Consumer Society*. London: Constable.

———. 1994. *On Aging*. Bloomington: Indiana University Press.

———. 1984. *Radical Humanism: Selected Essays*. Bloomington: Indiana University Press.

Anderson, Susan Heller. 1978. "Fania Fenelon: Musical Gift Meant Survival," *New York Times Biographical Service*. Pp. 42–43.

Arendt, Hannah. 1973. *The Origins of Totalitarianism*. New York: Harcourt Brace Jovanovich.

———. 1978. *The Life of the Mind*. New York: Harcourt Brace Jovanovich.

Aristotle. 1956. *On Poetry and Music*, translated by S. H. Butcher. New York: Macmillan Publishing Company.

Bakhtin, Mikhail. 1981. *The Dialogic Imagination: Four Essays*, edited by Michael Holquist, translated by Caryl Emerson and Michael Holquist. Austin: University of Texas Press.

———. 1984. *Rabelais and His World*, translated by Helene Iswolsky. Bloomington: Indiana University Press.

———. 1986. *Speech Genres and Other Late Essays*, edited by Caryl Emerson and Michael Holquist, translated by Vern W. McGee. Austin: University of Texas Press.

Bauer, Dale. 1991. "Gender in Bakhtin's Carnival." Pp. 671–84 in *Feminisms: An Anthology of Literary Theory and Criticism*, edited by Robyn R. Warhol and Diane Price Herndl. New Brunswick, New Jersey: Rutgers University Press.

Bauer, Dale and S. Jaret McKinstry, editors. 1991. *Feminism, Bakhtin, and the Dialogic.* Albany: State University of New York Press.

Bellow, Saul. 1970. *Mr. Sammler's Planet.* New York: Penguin Books.

Benhabib, Selya. 1986. *Critique, Norm, and Utopia: A Study of the Foundations of Critical Theory.* New York: Columbia University Press.

———. 1992. *Situating the Self: Gender, Community and Postmodernism in Contemporary Ethics.* New York: Routledge.

Benjamin, Walter. 1968. *Illuminations*, translated and with an introduction by Hannah Arendt. New York: Harcourt, Brace & World.

Berger, Peter L. and Thomas Luckmann. 1966. *The Social Construction of Reality: A Treatise in the Sociology of Knowledge*, New York: Anchor Books, Doubleday.

Bettelheim, Bruno. 1960. "Foreword." Pp. v–xviii in Miklos Nyiszli, *Auschwitz: A Doctor's Eyewitness Account*, translated by Tiobere Kremer and Richard Seaver. New York: Arcade Publishing.

Bladick, Chris. 1990. *The Concise Oxford Dictionary of Literary Terms.* Oxford University Press.

Bohle, Bruce, editor. 1975. *The International Cyclopedia of Music and Musicians.* 10th edition. New York: Dodd, Mead & Company.

Buszko, Joseph. 1990. "Auschwitz." Pp. 107–19 in *Encyclopedia of the Holocaust*, edited by Israel Gutman. New York: MacMillan Publishing Company.

Cameron, Gillie, Mary Lagerwey and Gerald E. Markle. 1993. "Whirlwinds of Pain: An Analysis of Holocaust Diaries." Presented at the Annual Meetings of the North Central Sociological Association. Toledo, Ohio.

Charlesworth, Andres. 1994. "Contesting Places of Memory: The Case of Auschwitz." *Environment and Planning D: Society and Space.* 12:579–93.

Chaplin, Charles, director and producer. 1940. *The Great Dictator* [Film]. Hollywood, CA: United Artists.

Chicago, Judy. 1993. *The Holocaust Project: From Darkness into Light.* New York: Penguin Books.

Chodorow, Nancy. 1978. *The Reproduction of Mothering: Psychoanalysis and the Sociology of Gender.* Berkeley: University of California Press.

Ciardi, John. 1959. *39 Poems.* New Brunswick, New Jersey: Rutgers University Press.

Cohen, Elie A. 1973. *The Abyss: A Confession.* New York: W.W. Norton Company.

Costello, Jeanne. 1991. "Taking the 'Woman' out of Women's Autobiography: The Perils and Potentials of Theorizing Female Subjectivities." *Diacritics* 23(2–3):123–134.

Culler, Jonathan. 1982. *On Deconstruction: Theory and Criticism after Structuralism.* Ithaca, New York: Cornell University Press.

Czech, Danuta. 1990. *Auschwitz Chronicle: 1939–1945.* New York: Henry Holt and Company.

Danow, David K. 1995. *The Spirit of Carnival: Magical Realism and the Grotesque.* Lexington, Kentucky: University of Kentucky Press.

Delbo, Charlotte. (1965) 1968. *None of Us Will Return,* translated by John Githens. Boston: Beacon.

———. 1982. "Who Will Carry the Word?" Pp. 269–325 in *The Theatre of the Holocaust: Four Plays.* Edited by Robert Skloot. Madison: University of Wisconsin Press.

———. 1990. *Days and Memory,* translated by Rosette C. Lamont. Marlboro, Vermont: The Marlboro Press.

———. 1995. *Auschwitz and After,* translated by Rosette C. Lamont. New Haven, CT: Yale University.

———. 1997. *Convoy to Auschwitz: Women of the French Resistance.* Boston: Northeastern University Press.

Denzin, Norman K. 1989a. "Reading *Tender Mercies*: Two Interpretations." *Sociological Quarterly* 30(1):37–57.

———. 1989b. *Interpretive Biography.* New York: Sage Publications.

———. 1990. "Presidential Address on *The Sociological Imagination* Revisited." *Sociological Quarterly* 31(1):1–22.

———. 1991. *Images of Postmodern Society: Social Theory and Contemporary Cinema.* Newbury Park, California: Sage Publications.

———. 1992. "The Many Faces of Emotionality: Reading Persona." Pp. 17–31 in *Investigation Subjectivity: Research on Lived Experience,* edited by Carolyn Ellis and Michael G. Flaherty, editors. Newbury Park: Sage Publications.

Des Pres, Terrence. 1976. *The Survivor: An Anatomy of Life in the Death Camps.* New York: Oxford University Press.

Dilthey, Wilhelm. 1961. *Meaning in History: W. Dilthey's Thoughts on History and Society,* translated by H. P. Rickman. London: George Allen & Unwin Ltd.

Durkheim, Emile. (1912) 1965. *The Elementary Forms of Religious Life,* translated by Joseph Ward Swain. New York: Free Press.

———. 1965. *The Division of Labor in Society.* New York: Free Press.

Dwork, Deborah, and Robert Jan van Pelt. 1994. "Reclaiming Auschwitz." Pp. 232–51 in *Holocaust Remembrance: The Shapes of Memory,* edited by Geoffrey H. Hartman. Cambridge: Blackwell.

Dworkin, Andrea. 1994. "The Unremembered: Searching for Women at the Holocaust Memorial Museum." *Ms.* November / December. 52–58.

Edelstein, Dov. 1984. *Worlds Torn Asunder.* New York: Ktav.

Elon, Amos. 1993. "The Politics of Memory." *The New York Review of Books* October 7, 1993: 3–5.

Ellis, Carolyn, and Michael G. Flaherty, editors. 1992. *Investigation Subjectivity: Research on Lived Experience.* Newbury Park: Sage Publications.

Ellis, Carolyn, and Arthur P. Bochner. 1996. "Introduction: Talking Over Ethnography." Pp. 13–45 in *Composing Ethnography: Alternative Forms of Qualitative Writing*, Carolyn Ellis and Arthur P. Bochner, editors. Walnut Creek, California: AltaMira Press.

Erben, Michael. 1993. "The Problem of Other Lives: Social Perspectives on Written Biography." *Sociology: The Journal of the British Sociological Association* 27(1):15–26.

Evans, Mary. 1993. "Reading Lives: How the Personal Might be Social." *Sociology: The Journal of the British Sociological Association* 27(1):5–13.

Feldman, Yael. 1992. "Whose Story is it Anyway? Ideology and Psychology in the Representation of the Shoah in Israeli Literature." Pp. 223–239 in *Probing the Limits of Representation: Nazism and the "Final Solution,"* edited by Saul Frielander. Cambridge: Harvard University Press.

Fenelon, Fania. (1976, 1977) 1981. *Playing for Time*, translated by Judith Landry. New York: Athenaeum.

———. 1976, 1979. *The Musicians of Auschwitz.* London: Sphere Books.

Fine, Ellen S. 1990. "Women Writers and the Holocaust." Pp. 79–95 in *Reflections of the Holocaust in Art and Literature*, edited by Randolph L. Braham. New York: Columbia University Press.

FirstSearch (July 1984 –). *Biography Index.* [MRDF]. Bronx, New York: H. W. Wilson. Available: Online Computer Library Center (OCLC). (paper version 1946–).

FirstSearch *Book Review Digest* (January 1983 –). [MRDF]. Bronx, New York: H. W. Wilson. Available: Online Computer Library Center (OCLC).

FirstSearch *Periodical Abstracts* (1986 –). [MRDF]. Louisville, Kentucky: UMI. Available: Online Computer Library Center (OCLC).

FirstSearch (1000 –) *WorldCat* [MRDF]. Dublin, Ohio: Available: Online Computer Library Center (OCLC).

Foucault, Michel. 1980. *Power and Knowledge.* New York: Pantheon.

Frank, Anne. (1947, 1967) 1995. *Diary of a Young Girl*, translated by B. M. Mooyaart. Garden City, New York: Doubleday.

———. (1949) 1995. *Anne Frank's Tales from the Secret Annex*, translated by Ralph Manheim and Michel Mok. New York: Bantam Books.

Frank, Arthur W. 1995. *The Wounded Storyteller: Body, Illness, and Ethics.* Chicago: University of Chicago Press.

Fraser, Nancy. 1989. *Unruly Practices: Power, Discourse and Gender in Contemporary Social Theory.* Minneapolis: University of Minnesota Press.

Friedrich, Otto. 1994. *The Kingdom of Auschwitz.* New York: Harper Perennial.

Gardiner, Michael. 1992. *The Dialogics of Critique: M. M. Bakhtin and the Theory of Ideology.* New York: Routledge.

Gergen, Mary M., and Kenneth J. Gergen. 1993. "Narratives of the Gendered Body in Popular Autobiography." Pp. 191–218 in *The Narrative Study of Lives*, edited by Ruthellen Josselson and Amia Lieblich. Newbury Park, California: Sage.

Goffman, Erving. 1961. *Asylums: Essays on the Social Situation of Mental Patients and Other Inmates*. Chicago: Aldine.

Goldenberg, Myrna. 1990. "Different Horrors, Same Hell: Women Remembering the Holocaust." Pp. 150–166 in *Thinking the Unthinkable: Meanings of the Holocaust*, edited by Roger S. Gottlieb. New York: Paulist Press.

Goodrich, Frances, and Albert Hackett. 1958. *The Diary of Anne Frank*. play and book club edition. New York: Random House.

Griswold, Wendy. 1994. *Cultures and Societies in a Changing World*. Thousand Oaks, California: Pine Forge Press.

Gutman, Yisrael, and Berenbaum, Michael. 1994. *Anatomy of the Auschwitz Death Camp*. Bloomington: Indiana University Press.

Hartman, Geoffrey H. 1993. "Public Memory and Modern Experience." *The Yale Journal of Criticism*. 6(2):239–47.

Hausknecht, Murray. 1990. "Bensonhurst and Auschwitz." *Dissent*. 37:100–01.

Heilbrun, Carolyn G. 1988. *Writing a Woman's Life*. New York: Norton.

Heinemann, Marlene E. 1981. *Women Prose Writers of the Nazi Holocaust*. Ph.D. Dissertation, Indiana University.

———. 1986. *Gender and Destiny: Women Writers and the Holocaust*. New York: Greenwood Press.

Herndl, Diane Price. 1991. "The Dilemmas of a Feminine Dialogic." Pp. 7–24 in *Feminism, Bakhtin, and the Dialogic*, edited by Dale. M. Bauer and S. Jaret McKinstry. Albany: State University of New York Press.

Hilberg, Raul. 1988. "I was not there." Pp. 17–25 in *Writing and the Holocaust*, edited by Berel Lang. New York: Holmes and Meier.

———. 1992. *Perpetrators Victims Bystanders: The Jewish Catastrophe, 1933–1945*. New York: HarperCollins.

Hill, Michael R. 1993. *Archival Strategies and Techniques*. New York: Sage Publications.

Holquist, Michael. 1986. *Dialogism: Bakhtin and his World*. New York: Routledge.

Horkheimer, Max. 1974. *The Eclipse of Reason*. New York: Seabury.

Horkheimer, Max, and Theodor Adorno. 1974. *The Dialectics of Enlightenment*. New York: Seabury.

Horowitz, Sara. 1997. *Voicing the Void: Mutness and Memory in Holocaust Fiction*. Albany: State University of New York Press.

Howe, Irving. 1976. *World of Our Fathers*. New York: Harcourt Brace Jovanovich.

———. 1988. "Writing and the Holocaust." Pp. 175–99 in *Writing and the Holocaust*, edited by Berel Lang. New York: Holmes & Meier Publishers, Inc.

Hutcheon, Linda. 1988. *A Poetics of Postmodernism: History, Theory, Fiction.* New York: Routledge.

———. 1989a. *The Politics of Postmodernism.* New York: Routledge.

———. 1989b. "Modern Parody and Bakhtin." Pp. 87–103 in *Rethinking Bakhtin: Extensions and Challenges*, edited by Gary Saul Morson and Caryl Emerson. Evanston, Illinois: Northwestern University Press.

———. 1993. "Beginning to Theorize Postmodernism." Pp. 243–272 in *A Postmodern Reader*, edited by Joseph Natoli and Linda Hutcheon. Albany: State University of New York Press.

Jameson, Fredric. 1981. *The Political Unconscious: Narrative as a Socially Symbolic Act.* Ithaca, New York: Cornell University Press.

Katz, Esther, and Joan Miriam Ringelheim. 1983. *Proceedings of the Conference, Women Surviving the Holocaust.* New York: Institute for Research in History.

Ka-Tzetnik 135633. (1963) 1987. *Moni*, originally published in the United States as *Atrocity*. Secaucus, New Jersey: Citadel Press.

Kielar, Wieslaw. *Anus Mundi.* 1980. New York: Times Books.

Kingcaid, Renee A. 1984. "Charlotte Delbo's *Auschwitz Et Apres*: The Struggle for Signification." *French Forum* 9(1):98–109.

Kor, Eva. 1992. Personal Communication. Kalamazoo, Michigan.

Krakowski, Shmuel. 1990. "Death Marches." Pp. 348–354 in *Encyclopedia of the Holocaust*, edited by Israel Gutman. New York: MacMillan Publishing Company.

Kurlansky, Mark. 1994. "Visiting Auschwitz." *Partisan Review.* LXI(2):234–39.

Lagerwey, Mary. 1994a. "Gold-Encrusted Chaos: Memoirs of Auschwitz." Doctoral Dissertation. Kalamazoo: Western Michigan University.

———. 1994b. "From Monologism to Chaos: Memoirs from Auschwitz." Presented at the British Sociological Association's Auto/Biography Annual Conference, University of Manchester, December 20–22, 1994.

Laks, Szymon. 1976. *Epizody, Epigramy, Esistoly.* London: Oficyna Poetow i Malarzy.

———. (1948) 1989. *Music of Another World*, translated by Chester Kisiel. Evanston, Illinois: Northwestern University Press.

———. 1990. "Orchestra of the Doomed: Memories of Conducting the Music of Auschwitz." Pp. B1, B4. *Washington Post.* April 8, 1990.

Lamont, Rosette. 1990. "Preface." Pp. vii–x in *Days and Memory*, by Charlotte Delbo. Marlboro, Vermont: Marlboro Press.

Langer, Lawrence L. 1975. *The Holocaust and the Literary Imagination*. New Haven, CT: Yale University Press.

———. 1978. *The Age of Atrocity: Death in Modern Literature*, Boston: Beacon Press.

———. 1990. "Fictional Facts and Factual Fictions: History in Holocaust Literature." Pp. 117–29 in *Reflections of the Holocaust in Art and Literature*, edited by Randolph L. Braham. New York: Columbia University Press.

———. 1991. *Holocaust Testimonies: The Ruins of Memory*, New Haven, CT: Yale University Press.

———. 1993. "Memory's Time: Chronology and Duration in Holocaust Testimonies." *Yale Journal of Criticism* 6(2):263–73.

———. 1995. "Introduction." Pp. ix–xviii in *Auschwitz and After,* Charlotte Delbo. New Haven, CT: Yale University Press.

Lanzmann, Claude. 1985. *Shoah*. Hollywood: Paramount Home Video.

———. 1994 "Why Spielberg has Distorted the Truth." *Guardian Weekly*, April 3, 1994. P. 14. (translated from Le Monde, March 3, 1994, Pp. 14–15).

Lengyel, Olga. (1946) 1947. *Five Chimneys: The Stories of Auschwitz*, translated by Clifford Coch and Paul P. Weiss. New York: Ziff-Davis.

Levi, Primo. (1947) 1959. *Survival in Auschwitz: The Nazi Assault on Humanity*, translated by Stuart Woolf. New York: Collier Books, Macmillan Publishing Company.

———. 1965. *The Reawakening*, translated by Stuart Woolf. New York: Collier Books.

———. (1981) 1986. *Moments of Reprieve: A Memoir of Auschwitz*, translated by Ruth Feldman. New York: Simon & Schuster.

———. (1975) 1984. *The Periodic Table*, translated by Raymond Rosenthal. New York: Schocken Books.

———. (1986) 1988. *The Drowned and the Saved*, translated by Raymond Rosenthal. New York: Simon & Schuster.

Lewis, Kevin. 1991. "The Auschwitz Museum and the Clash of Memories." *The Christian Century*. January 23, 1991:75–77.

Linden, R. Ruth. 1993. *Making Stories, Making Selves: Feminist Reflections on the Holocaust*. Columbus: Ohio State University Press.

———. 1996. "The Life Boat is Fraught: Reflections on 'Thrown Overboard.'" Pp. 160–71 in *Composing Ethnography: Alternative Forms of Qualitative Writing*, Carolyn Ellis and Arthur P. Bochner, editors. Walnut Creek, California: AltaMira Press.

Lindwer, Willy. 1988. *The Last Seven Months of Anne Frank*, translated by Alison Meerschaert. New York: Doubleday.

Lowenthal, David. 1985. *The Past is a Foreign Country*. Cambridge: Cambridge University Press.

Lyotard, Jean-Francois. (1979) 1984. *The Postmodern Condition: A Report on Knowledge*, translated by Geoff Bennington and Brian Fassumi. Minneapolis: University of Minnesota Press.

———. 1990. *Heidegger and "the jews"* translated by Andreas Michel and Mark S. Roberts, foreword by David Carrol. Minneapolis: University of Minnesota Press.

McCabe, Allyssa. 1991. "Preface: Structure as a Way of Understanding." Pp ix–xvii in *Developing Narrative Structure*, edited by Allyssa McCabe and Carole Peterson. Hillsdale, New Jersey: Lawrence Erlbaum Associates.

Markle, Gerald E. 1995. *Meditations of a Holocaust Traveler*. Albany: State University of New York Press.

Markle, Gerald E., Mary Lagerwey, Todd A. Clason, Jill A. Green and Tricia L. Meade. 1992. "From Auschwitz to Americana: Texts of the Holocaust." *Sociological Focus* 25(3):179–202.

Martelle, Scott. 1992. *Precious Memories.* Pp. 1C, 4C in *The Detroit News.* April 4, 1992.

Martineau, Harriet. 1853. *Biographies and Criticism of Comte.* London: G. Bell & Sons.

Mauriac, Francois. (1956) 1989. "Foreword," translated by Stella Rodway. Pp. vii–xi in *Night*, by Elie Wiesel. New York: Hill & Wang.

Mayotola, Gabriel. 1995. "Miserable Human Merchandise: Women of the Holocaust." *Mainstream* XXXXI (4):34–36.

Meade, Patricia L. 1992. "Gender Differences in Holocuast Autobiographies from Auschwitz. Unpublished Senior Honors Thesis. Kalamazoo, Michigan: Western Michigan University.

Merton, Robert. 1977. *The Sociology of Science in Europe.* Carbondale: Southern Illinois University Press.

Mestrovic, Stjepan G. 1988. *Emile Durkheim and the Reformation of Sociology.* Totowa, New Jersey: Rowman & Littlefield.

Miller, Arthur. 1978. *The Music of Auschwitz* New York: Carousel Films and CBS News.

Miller, Nancy K. 1991. *Getting Personal: Feminist Occasions and Other Autobiographical Acts.* New York: Routledge.

———. 1994. "Representing Others: Gender and the Subjects of Autobiography." *Differences: A Journal of Feminist Cultural Studies* 6(1): 1–27.

Mills, C. Wright. 1959. *The Sociological Imagination.* New York: Oxford University Press.

Milton, Sybil. 1984. "Women and the Holocaust: The Case of German and German-Jewish Women." Pp. 297–333 in *When Biology Became Destiny*, edited by Tenate Bridenthal, Atina Grossmann and Marion Kaplan. New York: Monthly Review Press.

Molodowsky, Kadia. 1976. Quoted in *World of Our Fathers*. Irving Howe. New York: Harcourt Brace Jovanovich.

Muller, Filip. 1979. *Eyewitness Auschwitz: Three Years in the Gas Chambers,* translated by Susanne Flatauer. New York: Stein and Day.

Netherlands State Institute for War Documentation. 1989. *The Diary of Anne Frank: The Critical Edition,* translated by Arnold J. Pomerans and B. M. Mooyaart, edited by Harry Paape, Gerrold Van Der Stroon and David Barnouw. New York: Doubleday.

Newman, Judith Sternberg. (1963) 1978. *In the Hell of Auschwitz: The Wartime Memoirs of Judith Sternberg Newman.* New York: Exposition Press.

Nomberg-Przytyk, Sara. 1985a. *Auschwitz: True Tales from a Grotesque Land,* translated by Roslyn Hirsch. Chapel Hill: University of North Carolina Press.

———. 1985b. *Esther's First Born,* translated by Roslyn Hirsch. Austin: Amor Fati.

Nyiszli, Miklos. (1960) 1978. *Auschwitz: A Doctor's Eye-Witness Account,* translated by Tibere Kremer and Richard Seaver, with a foreword by Bruno Bettelheim. London: Mayflower.

Ozick, Cynthia. 1983. *The Cannibal Galaxy.* Harmondsworth: Penguin.

———. 1988. "Roundtable Discussion." Pp. 277–284 in *Writing and the Holocaust,* edited by Berel Lang. New York: Holmes & Meier Publishers, Inc.

Patterson, David. 1992. *The Shriek of Silence: A Phenomenology of the Holocaust Novel.* Lexington: University Press of Kentucky.

Pawelczynska, Anna. 1979. *Values and Violence in Auschwitz: A Sociological Analysis.* Berkeley: University of California Press.

Perl, Gisella. 1984. *I Was A Doctor at Auschwitz.* Salem, New Hampshire: Ayer.

Personal Narratives Group. 1989. "Conditions not of Her own Making." Pp. 19–23 in *Interpreting Women's Lives: Feminist Theory and Personal Narratives,* edited by the Personal Narratives Group. Bloomington and Indianapolis: Indiana University Press.

Piper, Franciszek. 1994. *Auschwitz: How Many Perished: Jews, Poles, Gypsies....* Osciecim: Franciszek Piper.

Plath, Sylvia. 1962. "Daddy." Pp. 2207–08 in *The Norton Anthology of Literature by Women,* edited by Sandra Ml Gilbert and Susan Gubar. New York: W. W. Norton & Company.

Porter, Jack Nusan, editor. 1992. *The Sociology of Genocide/ The Holocaust: A Curriculum Guide.* Washington, D.C.: American Sociological Association (ASA) Teaching Resources Center.

Prince, Gerald. 1992. *Narrative as Theme.* Lincoln: University of Nebraska Press.

Quinney, Richard. 1996. "Once My Father Traveled West to California." Pp. 357–82 in *Composing Ethnography: Alternative Forms of Qualitative Writing,* Carolyn Ellis and Arthur P. Bochner, editors. Walnut Creek, California: AltaMira Press.

Reissman, Catherine Kohler. 1993. *Narrative Analysis.* New York: Sage Publications.

Richardson, Laurel. 1994. "Nine Poems: Marriage and the Family." *Journal of Contemporary Ethnography.* 23 (1):3–13.

———. 1996a. "Speech Lessons." Pp. 231–39 in *Composing Ethnography: Alternative Forms of Qualitative Writing,* Carolyn Ellis and Arthur P. Bochner, editors. Walnut Creek, California: AltaMira Press.

———. 1996b. "Educational Birds." *Journal of Contemporary Ethnography.* 25(1):6–15.

Riffaterre, Michael. 1990. *Fictional Truth.* Baltimore: The John Hopkins University Press.

Ringelheim, Joan. 1984. "The Unethical and The Unspeakable: Women and The Holocaust." Pp. 69–87 in *Simon Wiesenthal Center Annual. Volume I,* edited by Alex Grobman. Chappaqua, New York: Rossel Books.

———. 1985. "Women and the Holocaust: A Reconsideration of Research." *Signs* 10:741–761.

———. 1990. "Thoughts about Women and the Holocaust." Pp. 141–149 in *Thinking the Unthinkable: Meanings of the Holocaust,* edited by Roger S. Gottlieb. New York: Paulist Press.

———. 1993. "Women and the Holocaust: A Reconsideration of Research." Pp. 373–418 in *Different Voices: Women and the Holocaust,* edited by Carol Rittner and John K. Roth. New York: Paragon House.

Rittner, Carol, and John K. Roth. 1993. "Preface" and "Prologue." Pp. xi–19 in *Different Voices: Women and the Holocaust,* edited by Carol Rittner and John K. Roth. New York: Paragon House.

Robbins, Bruce. 1992. "Death and Vocation: Narrativizing Narrative Theory." *PMLA* 107:38–50.

Rose, Phyllis. 1993. "Writing Our Own Lives." *Ms.* September/October:76–77.

Rosen, Norma. 1969. *Touching Evil.* New York: Harcourt, Brace & World.

———. 1992. *Accidents of Influence: Writing as a Woman and a Jew in America.* Albany: State University of New York Press.

Rosenfeld, Alvin. 1991. "Popularization and Memory: The Case of Anne Frank." Pp. 243–78 in *Lessons and Legacies: The Meaning of the Holocaust in a Changing World,* edited by Peter Hayes. Evanston, Illinois: Northwestern University Press.

Roth, Phillip. 1986. "A Man Saved by His Skills." *New York Times Book Review.* October 12, 1986:1, 40.

Rousset, David. 1947. *The Other Kingdom.* New York: Reynal & Hitchcock.

Rubenstein, Richard L. 1992. *After Auschwitz: History, Theology, and Contemporary Judaism.* 2nd edition. Baltimore: Johns Hopkins University Press.

Sadie, Stanley, editor. 1980. *The New Grove Dictionary of Music and Musicians.* vol. 10. London: Macmillan.

Schnabel, Ernst. 1958. *Anne Frank: A Portrait in Courage*, translated Richard and Clara Winston. New York: Harcourt.

Siebert, Rudolf J. 1992. "From Habermas's Discourse Ethics to Benjamin's Political Theology: Anamnestic Solidarity." Paper presented at the annual meeting of the Michigan Academy of Science, Arts, and Letters, Central Michigan University.

Simon, Scott. 1995. "Weekend Edition/Saturday," produced by Cindy Carpien. Washington, D.C.: National Public Radio, March 11.

Smith, Sidonie. 1987. *A Poetics of Women's Autobiography*, Bloomington: Indiana University Press.

———. 1993. "Who's Talking/Who's Talking Back? The Subject of Personal Narrative." *Signs* 18(2):392–407.

Smith, Sidonie, and Julia Watson. 1992. *De/Colonizing the Subject: The Politics of Gender in Women's Autobiography*. Minneapolis: University of Minnesota Press.

Stanley, Liz. 1993. "On Auto/Biography in Sociology." *Sociology: The Journal of the British Sociological Association* 27(1):41–52.

Steiner, George. 1967. *Language and Silence: Essays on Language, Literature, and the Inhuman*. New York: Athenaeum.

Stevens, George. (1959) 1995. *Anne Frank: The Diary of a Young Girl*. movie and videocassette. Screenplay by Frances Goodrich, Albert Hackett. Beverly Hills: FoxVideo.

Stevenson, Sheryl. 1991. "Language and Gender in Transit: Feminist Extensions of Bakhtin." Pp. 181–98 in *Feminism, Bakhtin, and the Dialogic*, edited by Dale. M. Bauer and S. Jaret McKinstry. Albany: State University of New York Press.

Strivers, Camilla. 1993. "Reflections on the Role of Personal Narrative in Social Science." *Signs* 18(2):408–425.

Strzelecka, Irene. 1994. "Women." Pp. 393–411 in *Anatomy of the Auschwitz Death Camp*, edited by Yisrael Gutman and Michael Berenbaum. Bloomington: Indiana University Press.

Suchecky, Bernard. 1994. "The Carmelite Convent at Auschwitz: The Nature and Scope of a Failure." Pp. 160–73 in *Discourses of Jewish Identity in Twentieth Century France*, edited by Alan Astro. New Haven, CT: Yale University.

Sutzkever, Abraham. 1981. *Burnt Pearls: Ghetto Poems of Abraham Sutzkever*, translated by Seymore Mayne. Oakville, Ontario: Mosaic Press/Valley Editions.

Swindells, Julia. 1989. "Liberating the Subject? Autobiography and 'Women's History': A Reading of *The Diaries of Hannah Cullwick*." Pp. 24–38 in *Interpreting Women's Lives: Feminist Theory and Personal Narratives*, edited by the Personal Narratives Group. Bloomington and Indianapolis: Indiana University Press.

Sydie, Rosalind Ann. 1987. *Natural Women, Cultured Men: A Feminist Perspective on Sociological Theory*, New York: New York University Press.

Tec, Nechama. 1993. *Defiance: The Bielski Partisans.* New York: Oxford University Press.

Temple, Bogusia. 1994. "The Message and the Medium: Written and Oral Accounts of Lives." *Auto/Biography* (Lives and Works: Auto/biographical Occasions, Special Double Issue) 3(1) & 3(2):31–42.

Thomas, William Issac, and Florian Znaniecki. 1918. *The Polish Peasant in Europe and America.* Boston: Gorham Press.

United States Holocaust Memorial Museum Education Department. 1993. *Annotated Bibliography.* Washington, D.C.: United States Holocaust Memorial Museum.

van Pelt, Robert-Jan. 1994. "A Site in Search of a Mission." Pp. 93–156 in *Anatomy of the Auschwitz Death Camp*, edited by Yisrael Gutman and Michael Berenbaum. Bloomington: Indiana University Press.

van Pelt, Robert-Jan, and Deborah Dwork. 1996. *Auschwitz: 1270 to the Present.* New York: W. W. Norton & Company.

Weber, Max. 1949. *Max Weber on the Methodology of the Social Sciences*, translated and edited by Edward A. Shils and Henry A. Finch. Glencoe, Illinois: Free Press.

White, Hayden. 1987. *The Content of the Form: Narrative Discourse and Historical Representation.* Baltimore: The John Hopkins University Press.

———. 1992. "Historical Emplotment and the Problem of Truth." in *Probing the Limits of Representation: Nazism and the "Final Solution*, edited by Saul Friedlander. Cambridge: Harvard University Press.

Wiener, Wendy J., and Rosenwald, George C. 1993. "A Moment's Monument: The Psychology of Keeping a Diary." Pp. 30–58 in *The Narrative Study of Lives*, edited by Ruthellen Josselson and Amia Lieblich. Newbury Park, California: Sage.

Wiesel, Elie. (1958) 1960. *Night*, translated by Stella Rodway. New York: Hill & Wang.

———. 1978. *A Jew Today.* New York: Random House.

Wills, Clair. 1989. "Upsetting the Public: Carnival, Hysteria and Women's Texts." Pp. 131–51 in *Bakhtin and Cultural Theory.* Edited by Ken Hirschkop and David Shepherd. New York: Manchester University Press.

Young, James E. 1988. *Writing and Rewriting the Holocaust: Narrative and the Consequences of Interpretation.* Bloomington and Indianapolis: Indiana University Press.

———. 1991. "Israel's Memorial Landscape: Sho'ah, Heroism, and National Redemption." Pp. 279–304 in *Lessons and Legacies*, edited by Peter Hayes. Evanston, Illinois: Northwestern University Press.

———. 1993. *The Texture of Memory: Holocaust Memorials and Meaning.* New Haven, CT: Yale University Press.

Index

About the Author

Mary Lagerwey is an Assistant Professor of Nursing at Western Michigan University, where she teaches community health, qualitative research, and nursing ethics. She received her BA in sociology from Calvin College, her BS in nursing from Grand Valley State College, her MS in nursing from Michigan State University, and her PhD in sociology from Western Michigan University. She publishes in the areas of illness in fiction, gender studies, Holocaust studies, rural health, and the history of nursing ethics. She has also taught sociology at Western Michigan University and at Kalamazoo College.